In All Things of Nature There Is Something of the Marvelous.

__Aristotle__

GEMS OF THE NECKLACE

IMAGES OF THE CLEVELAND METROPOLITAN PARKS

PHOTOGRAPHS AND TEXT BY
GARY ALLEN MARMOLYA

FORWARD BY
ROBERT GLENN KETCHUM

Photographs Elite
Printed in
Cleveland, Ohio

To Mom and Dad
who allowed me to explore,
encouraged a sense of wonderment
about different cities, people, and places,
and who fostered respect for the land
and all living things upon it.

Copyright ©1993 Gary Allen Marmolya
Forward ©1993 Robert Glenn Ketchum

All rights reserved. Except for brief excerpts used by reviewers, no part of this publication may be used, reproduced, or copied by any means without the written permission of the publisher.

Library of Congress Catalog Number 93-092713
ISBN 1-883538-00-9

Published in the U.S.A.
Photographs Elite
12700 Lake Avenue,
Suite 2005
Lakewood, Ohio 44107
(216) 228-6640 or
(216) 521-9112

Produced in Cleveland, Ohio
Printed by Great Lakes Lithograph Company
Color Separations by Great Lakes Lithograph
Keylined by Sweet Impressions, Inc.
Concept and Design by Gary Allen Marmolya

The photography of Gary Allen Marmolya is represented by the Wach Gallery, Avon Lake, Ohio.
Lithographic reproductions of city skylines and natural landscapes are published by Photographs Elite.

Acknowledgements

The production of a book of this size and scope requires the help of many people. Though it was ultimately my job to pull together the many different facets of the project, there is no doubt that to reach the level of quality I sought, I needed the help, guidance, and talent of these people.

Michael Wilder whose extremely fine Cibachrome prints were used for the color separations. Michael has printed my work sinch 1988 and we have reached a working relationship where he can apply his many talents to create the image I invision. I often will create a photographic slide based on his printing abilities. For this book he spent many hours on the phone and reviewed copious notes about each image, resulting in finished prints that were consistently beautiful and perfectly executed.

Peter Wach who helped with the layout and design of *Gems of the Necklace*. Peter has been my mentor and agent in the realm of fine collectable photography since 1985. He first agreed to carry my work merely based on seeing my first poster *Eye of the Storm*. I may not have pursued serious photography without his enthusiasm and guidance. He is dedicated to the preservation and promotion of photography not only as an historical record, but as an art form.

The Cleveland Metropolitan Parks for making available the superb book by historian Carol Poh Miller, *Cleveland Metroparks, Past and Present*. Ms. Miller has created a detailed and extensive history of the park which was used as an important reference for many of the facts included in *Gems of the Necklace*. Also, thanks to the naturalists and nature center staffs for their advice and help throughout my own research and exploration.

Regan Fay of Jones, Day, Reavis & Pogue Attorneys for his empathy and guidance through the many barriers I never would have dreamed existed.

Kathleen Hempker for her enthusiastic support and who wrote a series of essays on the separate reservations, printed in *The Emerald Necklace*. This too was useful background information in building the structure of the text.

Ken Jordan a good friend and camera enthusiast who was very supportive throughout the various highs and lows of creating this book.

Lastly, for their dedication and hard work I want to thank my assistants (in italics) as well as others who have helped make this book a reality.

In alphabetical order:

Merces Canos, Michael Cicco, Dr. Rupert David, *Dianne Duffy*, Hildegarde Hull, Jennie Jones, Barb Keglovich, *Kathy Kehoe*, Anne Owens, Brittany Quay, Carole Schuerger, James Schultz, Carrie Spence, Jim Sprague, Richard Tunison, and Mary Urquhart.

Contents

Introduction   8
Forward   10
Emerald Necklace Maps   12

Huntington Reservation 14
Bradley Woods Reservation 22
Rocky River Reservation 30
Mill Stream Run Reservation 38
Big Creek Reservation 46
Hinckley Reservation 54
Brecksville Reservation 62
Bedford Reservation 70
Garfield Park Reservation 78
South Chagrin Reservation 86
North Chagrin Reservation 94
Euclid Creek Reservation 102
Metroparks Zoo 110

Artist's Statement   118
Technical Data   118

Explanation of Images:

Huntington Reservation 119
Bradley Woods Reservation 120
Rocky River Reservation 121
Mill Stream Run Reservation 122
Big Creek Reservation 123
Hinckley Reservation 124
Brecksville Reservation 125
Bedford Reservation 126
Garfield Park Reservation 127
South Chagrin Reservation 128
North Chagrin Reservation 129
Euclid Creek Reservation 130
Metroparks Zoo 131

Afterward   132
References   133

Spring Images	15	23	31	39	47	55	63	71	79	87	95	103	111
Summer Images	17	25	33	41	49	57	65	73	81	89	97	105	113
Fall Images	19	27	35	43	51	59	67	75	83	91	99	107	115
Winter Images	21	29	37	45	53	61	69	77	85	93	101	109	117

Introduction

The Cleveland Metropolitan Park System began in 1919 as a mere 3.8 acres of land in the northern part of what is now the Rocky River Reservation. It has grown to more than 19,000 acres of land composed of a chain of twelve park reservations as well as the Zoo. The reservations, collectively known as *The Emerald Necklace*, encircle downtown Cleveland while they they spread throughout Cuyahoga County and parts of four neighboring counties. They even extend a good distance south toward Akron, Ohio. Hence, virtually every segment of this region is but a short drive from the park. In many instances one can even drive from one reservation to another without leaving park land. Many Clevelanders refer to the park not as "The Emerald Necklace," but as "The Valley," because most the land follows stream and river beds below street level, or at the very least have within them ravines and gullies. Therefore, it's not unusual to hear someone say they are "going into the Valley." In any event, as a whole the park is a precious natural resource of unspoiled settings. It is the antithesis, yet compliment, to the city. Many Clevelanders find solace in just driving through the park, while others may have special niches they visit, which may be anything from a lookout point to just a special tree or rock. Even the Zoo, a different type of destination than the Emerald Necklace reservations, is built in a valley and is moderately wooded. People visit it as much to stroll the grounds as they do to see the animals.

It is this swath of green in and around Cleveland that I have relied so heavily on for many years, and I believe in some way has become a part of every Clevelander. I grew up on the west side of Cleveland, and as long as I can remember the park was a part of my life. It started out with picnics and exploration of the river bed of Rocky River. While in grade school I was fortunate to have lived on the edge of the park and would run home from school using the short cut through the "Valley" — one of several ravines leading into Rocky River. I learned the names of various trees and flowers, and constantly wanted to explore new hills and ravines. As I grew older the park became a place of both celebration as well as consolation through the various vicissitudes of life. I came to appreciate the land for just being there.

As a child, I would think about how the land must look much as it had hundreds of years ago, and I wondered what Indians may have traversed the same land or stood at a river bend to enjoy the same sights that I saw. Since then I have learned that the early Native American Indians and possibly the later Erie Indian Tribe did once inhabit this region. Consequently, I still have such ponderings, especially after compiling the text for *Gems of the Necklace* and finding that there are park lands that remain unaltered by humans. The remaining land has had an interesting and varied history over the past 200 years, but remains a natural setting for the continued growth and diversity of Nature's ways.

It is to this pristine quality of the park that this book is dedicated. Because it is an attempt to capture the spirit of the land it includes only natural scenes of beauty, scenes that will hopefully look very similar many years from now. Also, as every scene in some way includes images of trees, it is a reminder of their importance, not only to the ecology, but to our enjoyment of life. Images were chosen based on their inherent beauty and composition; art pieces that will stand the test of time anywhere in the country not as "Cleveland" scenes, but merely as Nature at her best.

While the book does contain factual information about the park, it is not meant to be a "tour book." There is no attempt to document landmarks, and many of the images could easily have been taken deep in the woods of any northern Ohio forest. However, within each reservation at least one image is a recognizable land formation in the area, and all four seasons are represented. Hopefully, over the course of each four images offered on a particular reservation a hint of the special ambience of the area will be apparent. At the same time I would encourage the readers to appreciate the images as representing a continuum of land which once engulfed the entire region.

Finally, I wish to point out that "Gems" refers not only to the special segments of the park system, but to the images within the book which might be considered the facets of any given gem. It also refers to the special moments found in the park, moments such as the glint of sunlight on a leaf or the special sounds heard along the way, moments that are not reproduceable but make all the difference in living life. These might be considered the shine added to the facets. All in all these things combine to form *The Emerald Necklace*.

A note on the layout of the book. The goal in creating *Gems of the Necklace* was not only to document the beauty of our parks, but to design and produce a book as an art piece in and of itself, designed to engage and keep pace with a reader from beginning to end. It is designed to flow much as a stream through the woods, with some uniformity but with changing patterns much as a stream might change course or glide over a rock. To help accomplish this there is a varying amount of open space throughout the book with only one objective per page, which the reader may consider worth stopping for or continue on to the next "site." For any given reservation in the book the information interspersed with the images is divided into statistics, maps, and history. While to some degree this might be considered a reference book, the information is meant primarily for the reader's enjoyment and to enhance the significance of each image. The accuracy of the information is no better than the references listed. Also keep in mind that for the greatest ease of reading, and due to space constraints, the park maps are not all of equal scale and the trails are shown for general positions only. I believe one could find most of the areas outlined without difficulty, but very accurate positions would require more detailed maps. Lastly, it must be kept in mind that there is much more to be learned about the reservations through the nature centers, historical societies, and libraries. In the meantime I hope you enjoy a stimulating learning and visual experience on your journey through *Gems of the Necklace*.

Gary Allen Marmolya

Forward

Great cities are distinguished by their foresight and planning, but most developed in an organic fashion, evolving and expanding as the economy allowed. Ultimately, it is some character of their design, or their unique setting that has immortalized them. Each has something incomparably attractive that makes us love to visit them. Ohio is a state endowed with great natural resources and beauty. In particular, the confluence of the river valleys and the rolling hillsides that define the landscape surrounding Cleveland have always been one of the city's greatest assests and attractions. Rich with wildlife, and accessibly close, the wooded folds welcome residents and visitors alike down into their meandering, richly forested river valleys to ponder the quiet passage of the water and the diverse melodies of songbirds.

Such a state of grace existed in many cities at the turn of the century and before, but in their quest for growth and stability they often sacrificed the very elements that made them appealing in the first place. The creation of park settings, inspired by designers and landscape "engineers," was a popular idea at the time. The penultimate example was Central Park in New York. Yet, already it was merely symbolic preservation of the last vestige of nature on Manhattan Island.

A great park does not come into existence without the foresight of someone who believes in its importance, and in turn, that person must rally the support of a community that will ultimately have to nurture and maintain it. As so often happens in the synchronicity of existence, Cleveland had such a person in William Stinchcomb, a young, self-taught engineer that recognized the need for open space in the future of the growing city. Capitalizing on some donations of river valley land, and with a design intended to incorporate all of the best known scenic spots, Stinchcomb proposed a series of parks at the far perimeters of the city that would be linked by the primary boulevards.

Guided by his input, the Cleveland Metropolitan Park District was born in 1917, and began the long and arduous process of trying to fulfill the planning ideal. It took time, money, and a public that was supportive, because without their commitment, nothing accomplished would last. But, support it they did, and unit by unit, sections were added. Popularly referred to as *The Emerald Necklace*, these park lands are one of the most significant attrations of the city, and an important refuge of its citizens. Down in the runs under the shade of trees, the damp cool is a welcome respite from the summer heat. In the fall, the remarkable deciduous forest puts on a show more grand and diverse in its variation than the woods of New England.

I was born, and have lived most of my life, in Los Angeles. Also, my photography has at one point or another taken me to many of the great cities of the world. Therefore, I have learned to appreciate the individual appeal of each city. To me, the urban centers that work the best and are the most enjoyable are those that have shown the most respect for their settings, and have integrated their natural landscape with the development of the city. In Los Angeles our integration with nature is abruptly at the edge of the city. Although we do have park lands, our gardens and domestic greenery suffice as most citizens' retreat. Manhattan "fenced in" what was left of their natural world, defining it as a few allocated acres, surrounded by a forest of concrete. Tokyo, Paris, London and most of the great capitals did similarly, basically creating park systems that were squeezed in amongst the spreading construction and destruction of urbanity. In this country, San Francisco and Cleveland stand out in my mind as being amoung the few that have successfully embraced and integrated their natural surroundings, realizing them as part of the essence of the city.

When I think back on my visit to a destination, my memory is defined by the particulars of that place that stands out. Although I can clearly recall the corporate architecture of downtown Cleveland, and the good mood floating in the warm air of a Friday night as thousands of people wander down into the flats to drink and eat, what I remember most are the gently rolling hills affording me an occasional view through the skein of trees. Walking amoung those trees resonates through my being, reviving me with the miracle that it represents. I can recall specific ones, and find them again when I return. I can also recall specific sounds, like the quiet swish of a branch so low on the water that small waves keep grabbing it and pulling it down into the stream for a moment's immersion. A marvelous memory it must be, indeed, because my mind has held on to it, long after forgetting "more inportant" things. That is the essence of the attraction.

What has been created with this park system is hard to define. There is no statistic of specific value, just attendance. Trees and streams do not equate as factors in an economic formula, giving absolute proof that they have "worth" other than for their extractable value. But, it is those very intangible qualities that linger longest in memory, and nurture the lives of those that live adjacent to their beauty. These parks are not an extractable resource in the traditional sense. The importance of them is the opportunity they afford all of us to interact with wildness and further our learning from nature through personal exploration, a much more enlightened form of extraction.

Here at the end of the 20th century, our nation is seeking a constant. We feel increasingly adrift and disconnected, and I believe it is because we have strayed so far from our understanding of life and living things. Our urbanity has removed most of us from a daily exchange with the natural world, and so we are increasingly disassociated from the very nature of our existence. We are loosing our appreciation of the diversity and wonder of life, and our sense of place (the understanding of where we live) is slipping away. The future will belong to those that can still comprehend the importance of maintaining that connection. It is cities like Cleveland, enhanced greatly by the existence of these parks, that seem best prepared for that future.

You have not only created an incredible recreational system for yourselves, but you have maintained and endowed it, even in the face of opposition and neglect. Now the reward is yours. Your city is graced by the Metroparks in a way few other cities in the world could ever even hope to approximate, and only now is the rest of the world beginning to realize the advantage of such a resource. May it serve you well, . . . and more importantly, may you serve it well.

Robert Glenn Ketchum

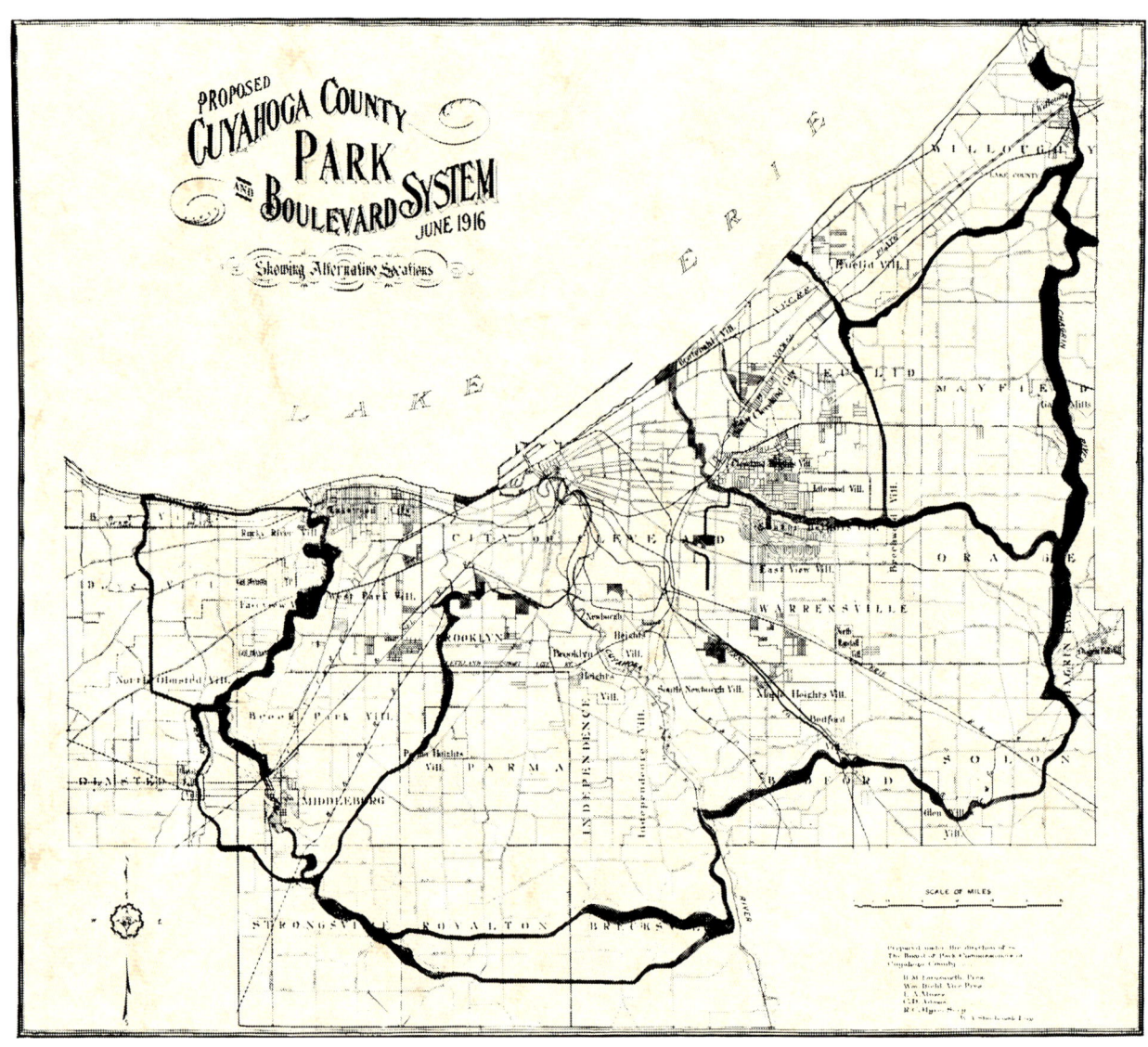

Map of 1916 shows land first planned for the Metropolitan Park System, a rim of parks and parkways throughout Cuyahoga County encircling downtown Cleveland. They would be only a short drive from anywhere in the county.

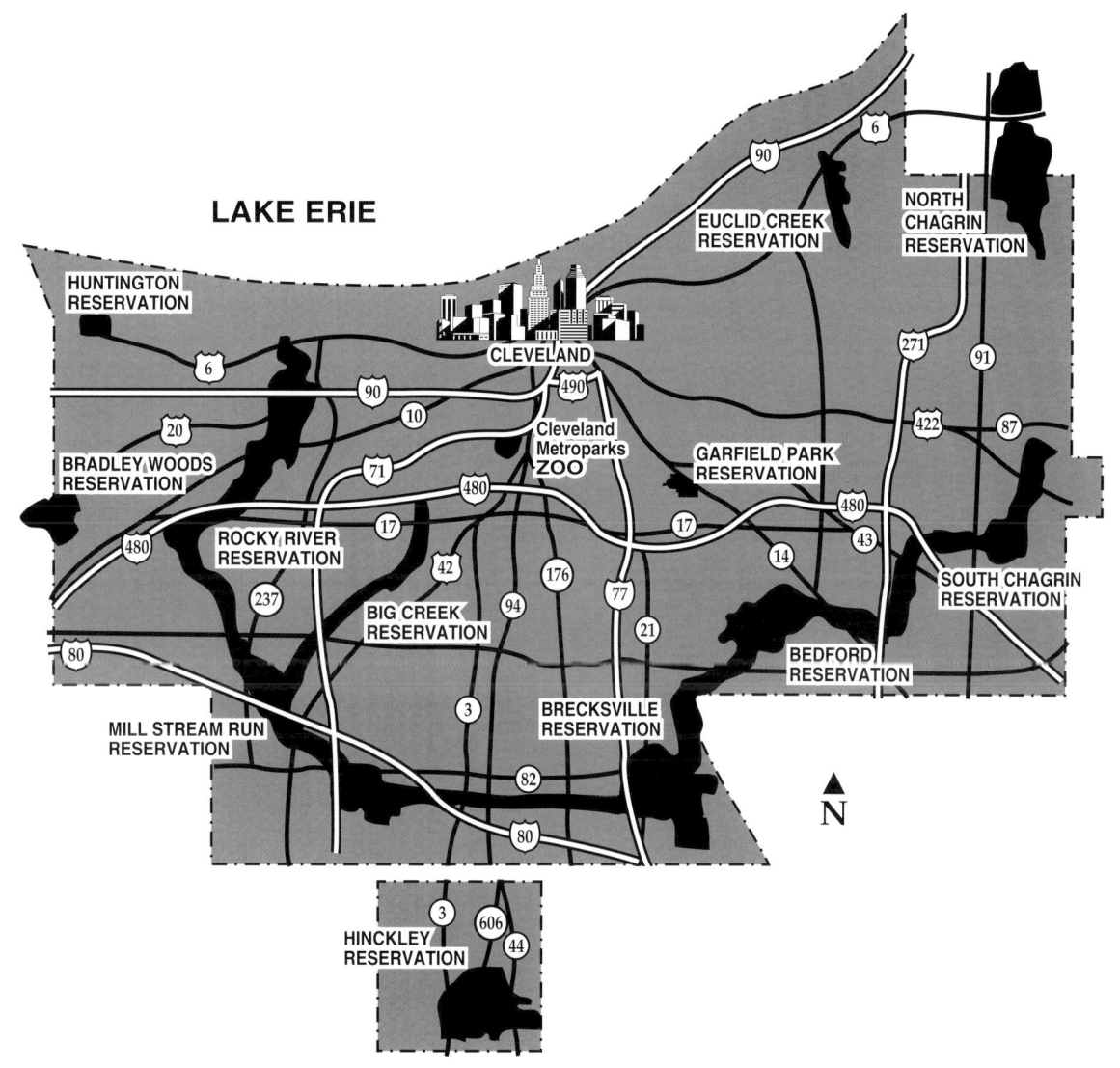

Current map shows land now in the park system (not to scale). It closely matches the original plan but now involves additional counties, most noticeably seen in the Hinkley Reservation, a distant southern extension of the *Emerald Necklace*.

Huntington Reservation

Acquired:	1926
Size:	100 Acres
Location:	16 miles west of downtown Cleveland
Features:	Lake Erie Nature and Science Center Baycrafters Art Studio Huntington Playhouse Gallery Shop Annual Renaissance Fair All-Purpose Trail Hiking Trail Baseball Diamond Swimming Fishing Sledding
Water Resource:	Lake Erie Porter Creek
Terrain:	Bluffs overlooking Lake Erie & wide beach Wooded bluffs and valley around Porter Creek Playing Fields

Huntington Reservation 15

Huntington Reservation

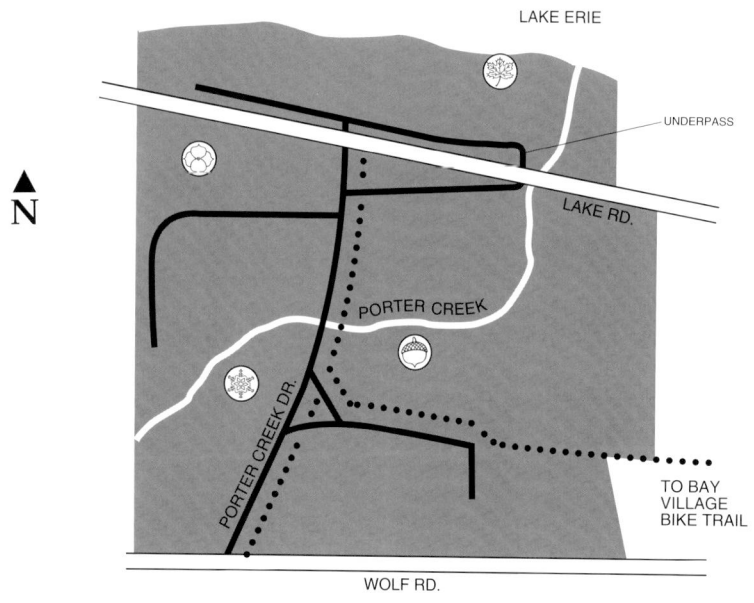

Huntington Reservation

Huntington Reservation

The only reservation to border Lake Erie, the land was once the country estate of John Huntington. Mr. Huntington emigrated from England in 1852. Starting in the roofing business, he went on to become a wealthy industrialist and held many patents in oil refining. After building his own oil refining business, he merged in 1870 with several refineries, including that of John D. Rockefeller, to form the Standard Oil Company. He was also involved in lake shipping and was a founder of the Cleveland Stone Company.

Often mistaken for a light house, a water tower still stands on the bluffs overlooking Lake Erie. The tower was built to hold a water tank filled with water pumped up from the lake. This in turn was used to irrigate Mr. Huntington's grape orchards. The tower is listed on the National Register of Historic Places.

Other interesting structures include the former Nickel Plate Railroad Station which houses the Baycrafters Art Gallery. Built in 1882, it was moved from the nearby Dover Center Crossing in 1963. Also of note is the Fuller House just behind the art gallery. Originally part of the Lawrence Estate, it eventually became part of the old Bayview Hospital complex and was moved by barge down the shores of Lake Erie in order to be relocated at it's present site!

Huntington Reservation

The beach well below the water tower has been popular for swimming since the 1920's. The stone piers and breakwall were built in 1929, and strengthened in 1948. Until the 1940's, the Lake Shore Electric Railway used to bring Clevelanders to the park. Huntington was stop 27 and the concrete trestles can still be seen in the woods surrounding Porter Creek. Monoliths celebrating another era, they stand their ground but are encroached upon by trees and vines.

There is a strong cultural art presence at Huntington. Of note is the Baycrafters Organization which was founded in 1948 for the encouragement and instruction in the arts and crafts. Also, there is the Huntington Playhouse which started out in a barn from the Huntington estate. In the fall, a very popular Renaissance Fair hosts numerous art and craft booths amidst entertainment and dress of this earlier period of history. These cultural events may be a perfect tribute to Mr. Huntington who gave a great part of his estate to the building of the Cleveland Museum of Art, completed in 1916.

Huntington Reservation 21

Bradley Woods Reservation

Acquired:	1960
Size:	780 Acres
Location:	17 miles west of downtown Cleveland
Features:	Waterfowl Sanctuary
	Large Deer Population
	Hiking Trail
	Baseball Diamond
	Fishing
	Ice Fishing
	Ice Skating
Water Resource:	Bunns Lake
Terrain:	"Swamp Forest"
	Flat

Bradley Woods Reservation

Bradley Woods Reservation

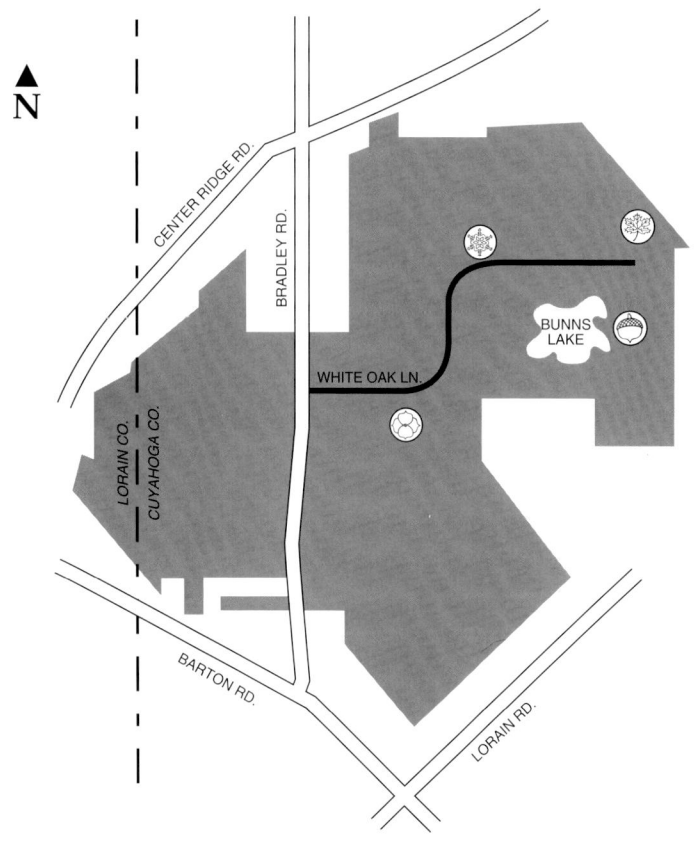

Bradley Woods Reservation

Bradley Woods Reservation

The first new reservation in over 30 years, Bradley Woods opened in 1962. Situated on a large Berea sandstone formation, it is very flat and supports what is considered a *Swamp Forest* due to the poor drainage. Early settlers called the heavily forested area South Bradley Woods. Early commercial aviation pilots used to orient themselves by the woods as it was the largest group of trees seen on the route between Cleveland and Detroit. At one time there were farm fields and orchards here. Because of heavy forest cutting in 1939, the trees seen today are small and close together. However, there are still some old sour gum, tulip, red maple, and sugar maple trees throughout the woods. The most abundant tree species are red maple and sour gum with a fair number of yellow-birch and pin oak also present.

Bradley Woods Reservation

The sandstone beneath Bradley Woods was once quarried by several companies early in the century. The fine grade of sandstone was used for mill and grind stones and can still be seen in several abandoned quarry sites

Bunns Lake was created in 1986 as a waterfowl sanctuary and fishing spot. The area is a nesting site for various kinds of ducks and has been a long time haunt of bird enthusiasts, especially in the spring. But in addition to the numerous birds, there is a deer herd in Bradley Woods and one might also see a fox, raccoon, or one of several types of squirrels. Though it is the flattest terrain in *The Emerald Necklace* there are numerous paths through the woods surrounding Bunns Lake and picnic area. The widest paths extend south of the picnic shelter.

Bradley Woods Reservation

Rocky River Reservation

Acquired:	1919 — 1st Parcel of Land, North End
Size:	3,432 Acres
Location:	11 miles west of downtown Cleveland
Features:	Nature Center 3 Golf Courses Stinchcomb Memorial Frostville Museum Stables Bridle Trail Fishing Ice Fishing All-Purpose Trail Hiking Trail Physical Fitness Trail Baseball Diamond Sledding Boating/Boat Launch
Water Resource:	Rocky River Rocky River East Branch Rocky River West Branch West Channel Pond
Terrain:	Wide valley — north end Narrow valley — south end Shallow, meandering river Heavily wooded with large fields at north end

Rocky River Reservation 31

Rocky River Reservation

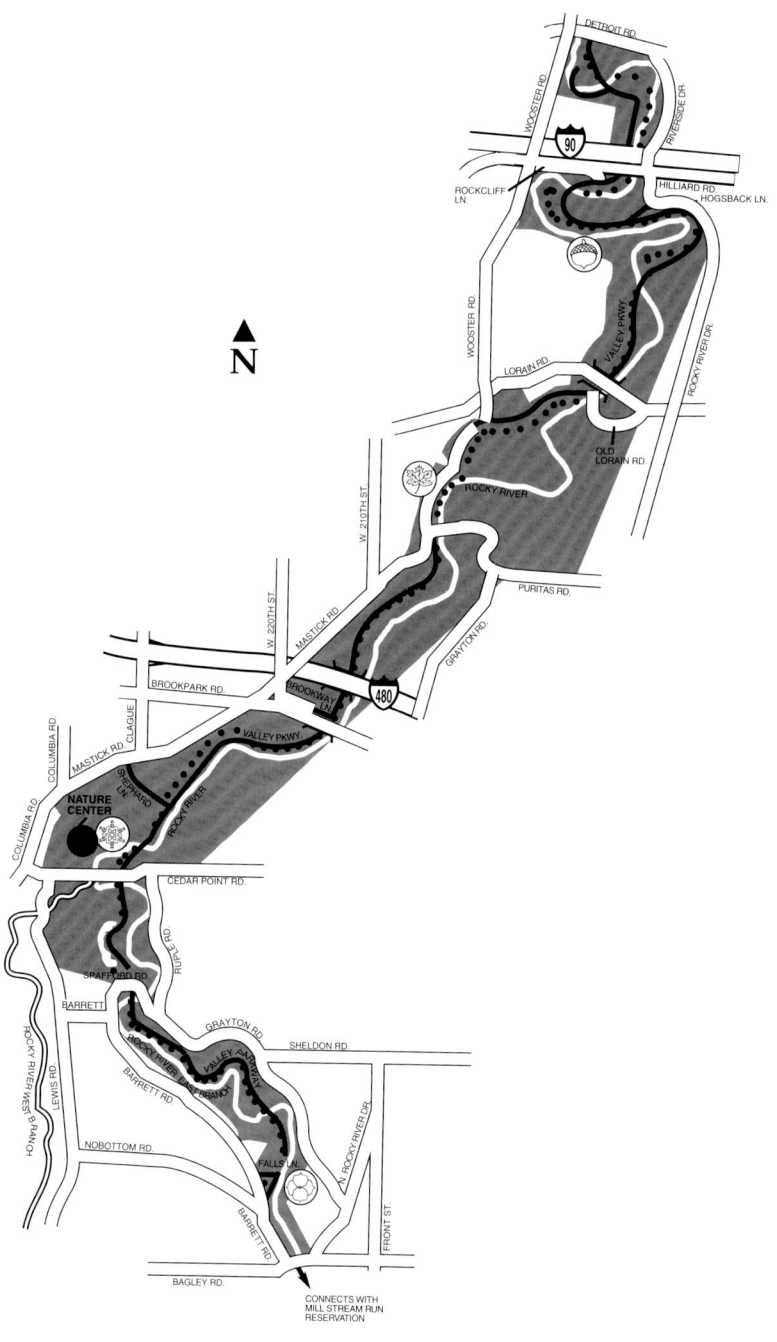

Rocky River Reservation

The Rocky River Reservation must be considered *The Original Gem.* The first land purchased by the park district was in 1919 in the northern end of this reservation. The park first acquired the ability to buy land in 1915. At this time, it was most interested in lands to the east and west of Cleveland because these were nearest to the city and in the path of the most rapid expansion. Hence, in October of 1915, the park had Frederick Law Olmsted, Jr., a landscape architect of national stature, explore the Rocky River Valley to advise on its possible development. This was one month after he had explored the Euclid Creek Valley to the east. Extremely impressed with the beauty of each, he recommended they be preserved as parks. Many other visitors have been impressed with the Rocky River Valley. It is said that General William T. Sherman when visiting Cleveland at the end of the Civil War compared the beauty of the valley to that of Old World landscapes.

This reservation is dominated by the meandering, shallow Rocky River which is about 12,000 years old. Prior to this, there was a wide, deep river valley once filled by glaciers and located east of the current basin. In several places, such as the Metroparks Golf Courses, the newer river crosses the old valley producing a broad based "U" shaped basin of an older river. Most of the glacial debris has been washed downstream into Lake Erie, but large heavy granite boulders and smaller rocks remain; hence, the name Rocky River.

Rocky River Reservation

At the southern end of the reservation, the East and West Branches of Rocky River merge at the base of Cedar Point Hill and Fort Hill. These two hills were once connected by land that was eroded from both sides until the two rivers merged at a new site. The remining Fort Hill is 90 feet above the river on its east side, and the old river bed of the West Branch of Rocky River on its west side.

At the eastern premonitory of Fort Hill are three trenches and embankments once believed to be protection for a fort occupied by the Whittlesey Tradition Native Americans around 1000 to 1690AD. However, more recent archeological excavations have lead some to believe these very eroded embankments are even older, and may have served ritualistic purposes. The bottom land left by the old West Branch of Rocky River was considered a good area for early inhabitants to grow crops. It was dammed in 1974 to form a marsh for a greater array of wildlife.

A spectacular view of the northern valley is seen from the Stinchcomb Memorial. Built to honor the first park director, a man of great vision in shaping the park system. The memorial is on a grassy hill accessible by car. The plateau of the hill has a short walking path around its perimeter and is also a favorite site of sunbathers and kite flyers.

Rocky River Reservation

Mill Stream Run Reservation

Acquired: Dedicated 1976
Parts of Valley Parkway already in
    Park system before 1976
Land in Baldwin and Wallace Lake area
    acquired in 1937

Size: 2,307 Acres

Location: 16 miles southwest of downtown Cleveland

Features: Chalet
Toboggan Run
Camp Cheerful
Boating
Swimming
Bridle Trail
Fishing
Ice Fishing
All-Purpose Trail
Hiking Trail
Physical Fitness Trail
Baseball Diamond

Water Resource: East Branch of Rocky River
Ranger Lake
Baldwin Lake
Wallace Lake

Terrain: Wide valley with meadows and flood plain
Heavily wooded forest with deep ravines
    cut by three streams at south end

Mill Stream Run Reservation

Mill Stream Run Reservation

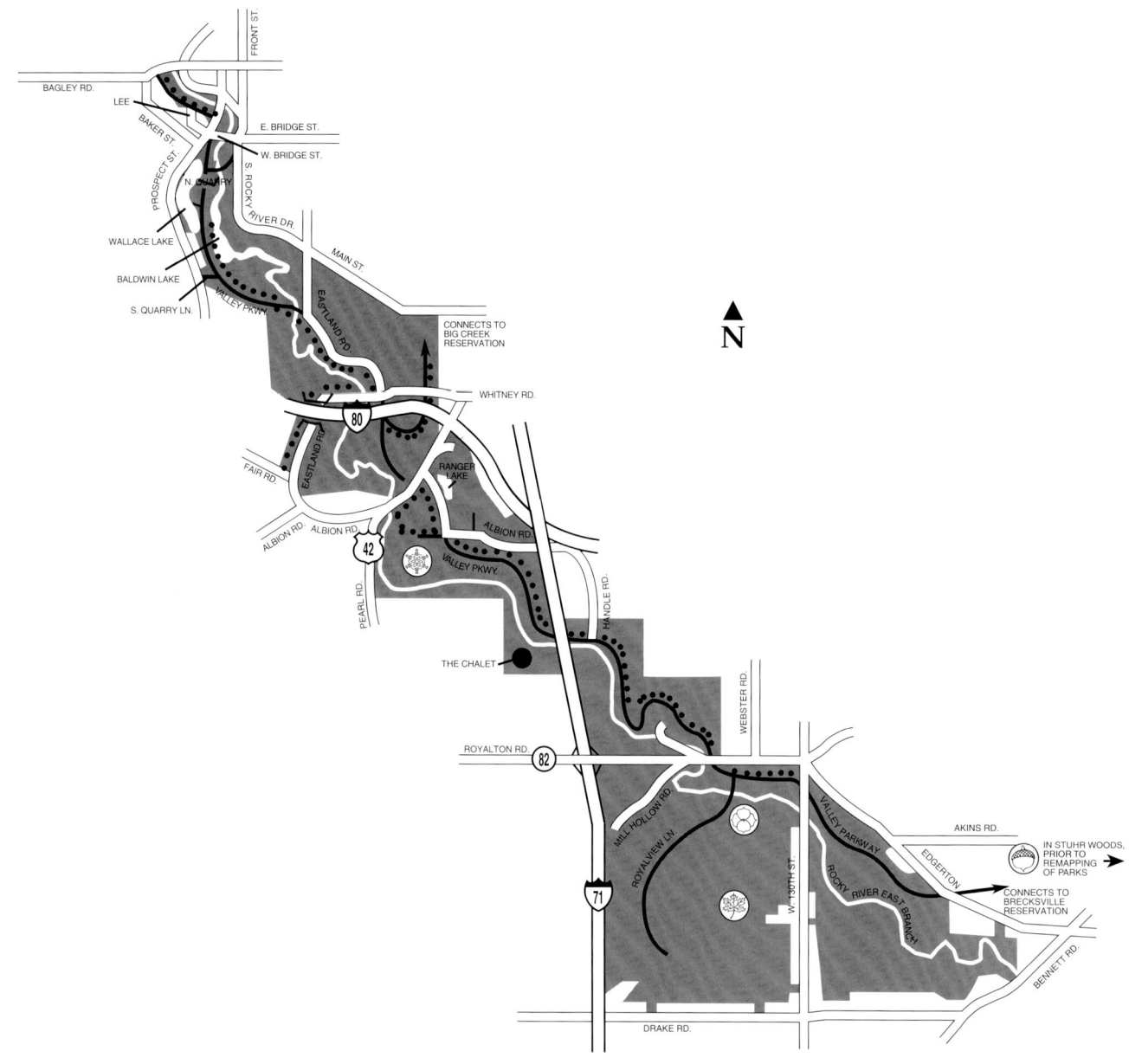

Mill Stream Run Reservation

Based on artifacts such as axes, hammers, and knives that have been found in this area it is believed that some of the earlier inhabitants were Native American Indians of 8,000 to 9,000 years ago. It is interesting to hypothesize that the water resource drew them here. We do know that the water power provided by the East Branch of Rocky River drew settlers here in the early 1800's. At that time, two communities once existed here. Sanderson's Corners had a saw mill, basket factory, and a carriage factory. It was located at the southern end of the reservation (at the corner of Drake and Hunt Roads). Another settlement, Slab Hollow, was named for slabs cut from logs at the saw mill. It also had a grist mill, blacksmith shop, schoolhouse, and small store.

What these communities didn't use they sold at markets in Lorain and Cleveland. The mills were active until the 1850's when steam engines allowed a greater choice of mill sites. Also, the roller process of milling flour eliminated the need for waterwheel grist mills using granite millstones.

Mill Stream Run Reservation

Baldwin and Wallace Lakes in what is now the north end of the reservation started out as sandstone quarries. After acquiring the land in 1937, the park system filled in some areas and dammed Rocky River to form Baldwin Lake. Then in 1942 Wallace Lake was created by flooding two additional quarries which were connected by a shallow basin. This part of the reservation was originally part of the Rocky River Reservation, but was remapped in 1992 to be included with Mill Stream Run.

Mill Stream Run has been farmed and forested in the past and some of the old fields are in the shrub stage of succession. There are also heavy woods of second growth trees with mature beech, maple, and oak in the ravines. Lastly, along the river and flat valley is a flood plain forest. Among the spring wildflowers supported by the flood plain are several vibrant stands of Virginia Bluebells which are easily seen from the trails. However, numerous other wildflowers, often with dense and colorful growth, are found throughout the entire reservation.

Mill Stream Run Reservation

Big Creek Reservation

Acquired:	1920's
Size:	443 Acres
Location:	8 miles southwest of downtown Cleveland
Features:	Lake Isaac Waterfowl Sanctuary All-Purpose Trail Hiking Trail Physical Fitness Trail Baseball Diamond Sledding
Water Resource:	Big Creek Lake Isaac Baldwin Creek
Terrain:	Long wooded ravine Several open fields Lake and marsh

Big Creek Reservation

Big Creek Reservation

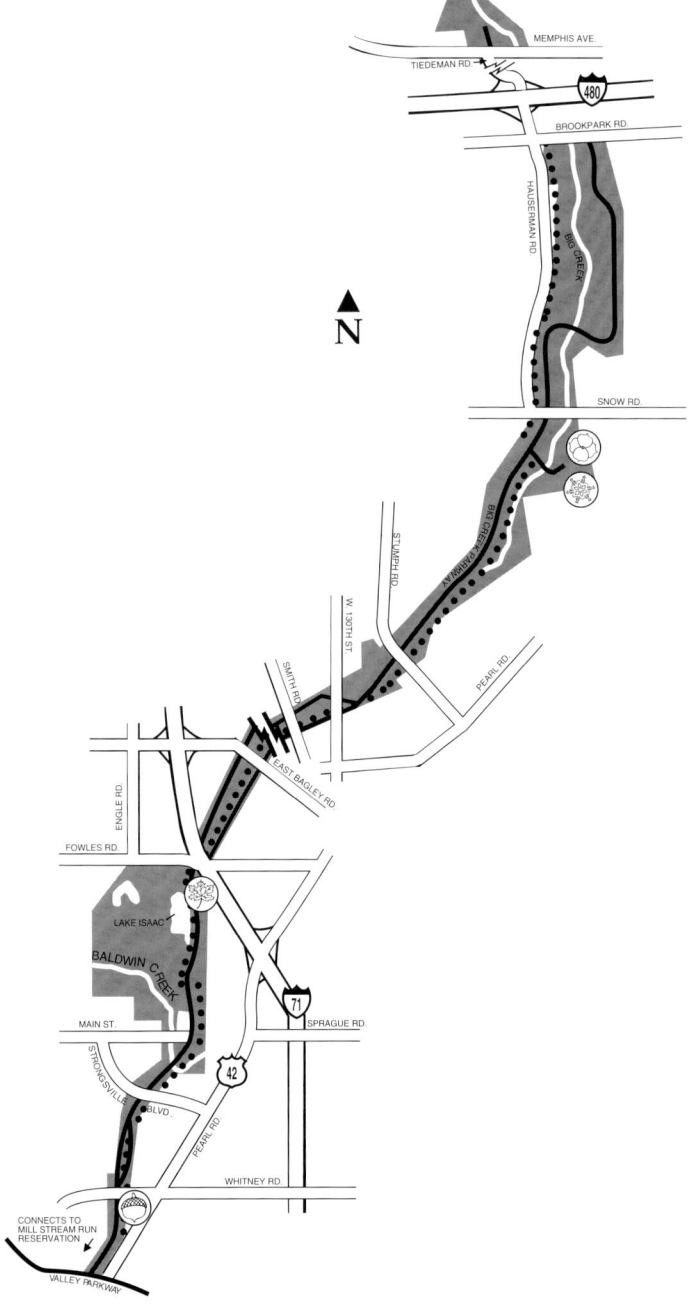

Big Creek Reservation

Big Creek Reservation

Once known as the Wooster Pike Connection, Big Creek Parkway was originally conceived in 1916 as a way to join Brookside Park (which was owned by the City of Cleveland) with the Rocky River Reservation. Not all the originally proposed land was acquired. Nevertheless, a seven mile long parkway now follows the course of Big Creek, which has carved an interesting ravine through the land. The southern portion of the parkway was built and landscaped by the WPA in the 1930's. At its southwestern end the parkway does indeed join what was once part of the Rocky River Reservation, an area remapped in 1992 as part of Mill Stream Run Reservation.

Big Creek Reservation

In the southern most portion of Big Creek Reservation is the Lake Isaac Waterfowl Sanctuary. Lake Isaac and its sister lake, Lake Abrams, are named after Isaac and Abram Fowles, early settlers in the area. Both lakes were created by leftover "pot holes" made by glaciers. However, Lake Isaac has also been enlarged by building a dam.

Since it is along the path of many migratory waterfowl using the Rocky River Valley migration corridor, up to 800 birds roost on Lake Isaac. Along the north side of the lake is a 100 acre tract of marsh, floodplain, woodlands, and orchard supporting not only the birds, but a large array of animal species. Some of the interesting animals found in the area include foxes, mink, deer, and opossums. The area is considered "one of the most active wildlife corridors in Cuyahoga County."

Big Creek Reservation

Hinkley Reservation

Acquired:	1920's
Size:	2,275 Acres
Location:	30 miles south of downtown Cleveland
Features:	Boating Swimming Repelling Worden Heritage Homestead Fishing Ice Fishing Bridle Trail All-Purpose Trail Hiking Trail Baseball Diamond Ice Skating Sledding
Water Resource:	Hinkley Lake Ledge Lake Judge's Lake East Branch of Rocky River
Terrain:	Broad valley Large lake near center Steep cliffs and ledges Thick woods

Hinkley Reservation

Hinkley Reservation

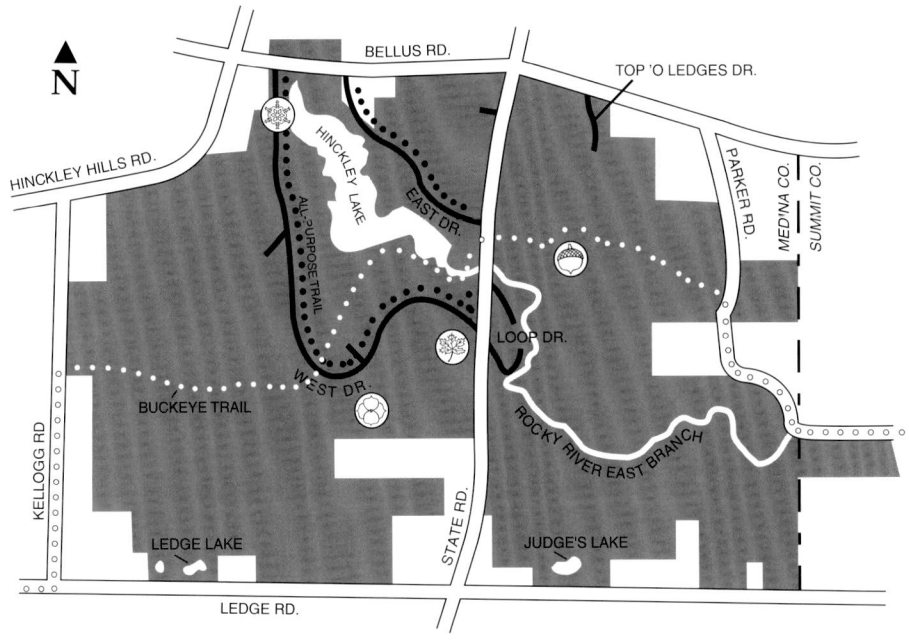

Hinkley Reservation

Hinkley Reservation

The Switzerland of America is what George Emmett called Hinkley in the early 1920's when he wanted it preserved in the Cleveland Metropolitan Park District. Another early contributor to the effort was John F. Johnson. Of the 236 acres he donated, 100 were converted into Hinkley Lake in 1925 by damming the East Branch of Rocky River.

Hinkley Lake is in a large valley excavated by two successive preglacial streams and then also excavated by the East Branch of Rocky River. Whipp's Ledges rise 350 feet above the lake exposing walls of Sharon Conglomerate. This is a porous sandstone created 250 million years ago during the coal age. It resulted from sand and quartz pebbles washed into a river delta and then cemented together. Because of the porous quality of these rocks, many nearby springs exist and vegetation covers many rocks. Some plants, such as the polypoid fern, are not found in other park reservations.

Just as Harry Church had carved figures in sandstone in the South Chagrin Reservation (p. 90), so did Hinkley Reservation have its sculptor. Noble Stuart was a bricklayer who carved images of a schooner, Ty Cobb, and a cross suspended over an open Bible, among others found in the soft sandstone. Of these carvings created in the 1940's it is said that the schooner represented his father's means of death, and that Ty Cobb, the famous baseball player, often went hunting and fishing with Mr. Stuart. Though the elements have taken their toll on some of the fine details, the carvings still exist behind the Worden House on land purchased by the Park in 1960.

Hinkley Reservation

The ledges are named after Robert Whipp who, after emigrating from England in 1848, acquired 2,000 acres of land in Hinkley Township. The ledges were part of his property. An interesting historical insight is that Mr. Whipp's second wife, who was 30 years younger than he was, tried to strangle him with the help of her lover and her brother. His wife and her brother were sent to jail, but there was no positive identification of the third person.

Ever since 1957 Hinkley has been known for the return of the buzzards with Buzzard Sunday celebration in late March. These are actually turkey vultures returning from their winter ranges in Kentucky, Tennessee, Virginia, and for some, as far away as South America. They ride warm updrafts and can be differentiated from hawks and falcons by their six-foot wing span. Folklore states they were attracted to the area in 1808 when a Wyandott squaw was hung for witchcraft. Another version claims they were attracted to Hinkley in 1819 after 400 settlers enclosed a 25-mile area and in order to protect their livestock killed hundreds of predators such as foxes and bears. It became know as the *Great Hinkley Hunt of December 1818*.

Of interest to hikers is the Buckeye Trail. The Medina segment of this state trail cuts across the Hinkley Reservation (p. 56). In Whipp's Ledges the trail follows the *Hallway* (p. 59) where, with park permission, rock climbers practice their skills. On its way north it passes through the Brecksville (p. 64, 68), Bedford (p. 72, 76), South Chagrin (p. 88, 92), and North Chagrin (p. 96, 98) Reservations.

Hinkley Reservation

Brecksville Reservation

Acquired:	1920's
Size:	3,090 Acres
Location:	14 miles south of downtown Cleveland
Features:	Nature Center Squire Rich House & Museum Golf Course Stables Bridle Paths All-Purpose Trail Hiking Trail Physical Fitness Trail Baseball Diamond Sledding
Water Resource:	Chippewa Creek
Terrain:	Rolling hills and deep ravines Heavily wooded Several open fields Chippewa Creek Gorge

Brecksville Reservation

Brecksville Reservation

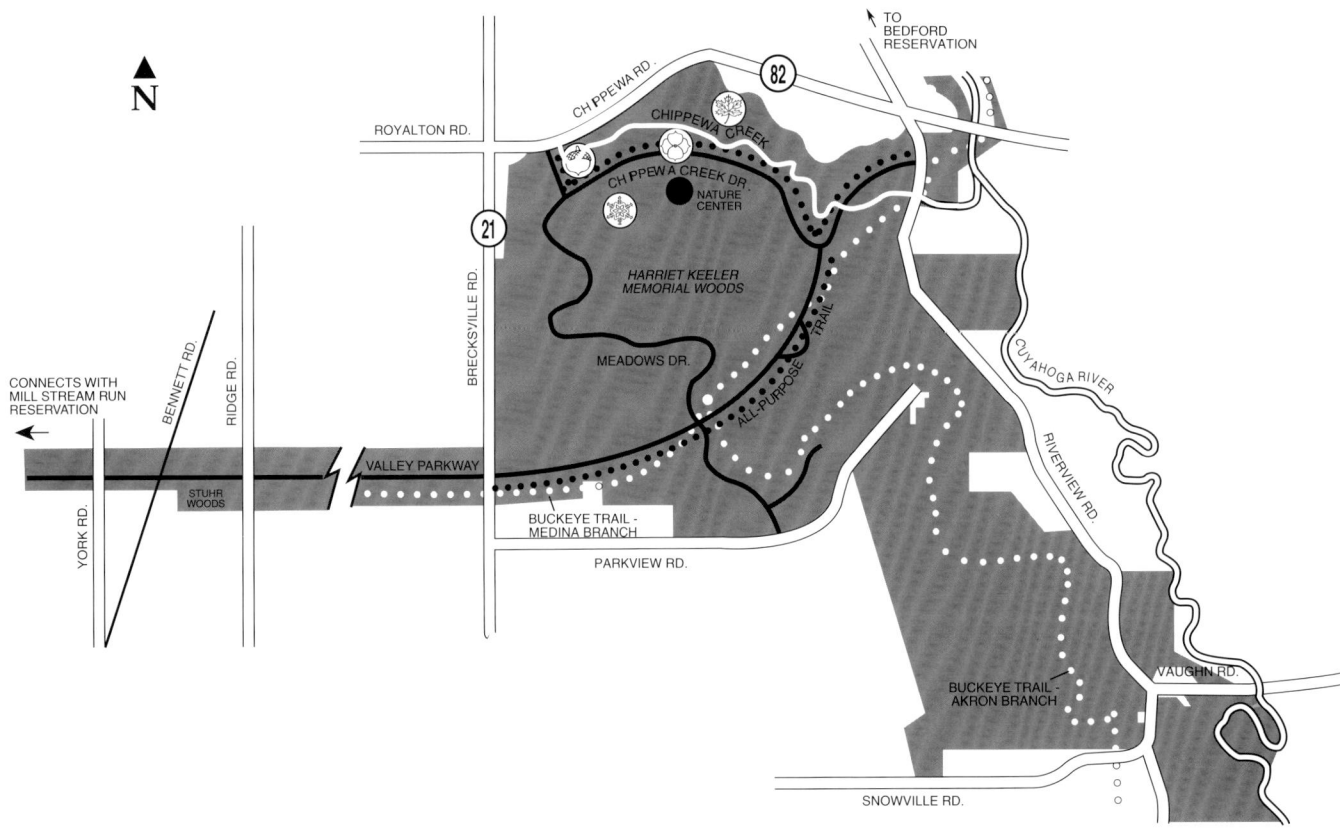

Brecksville Reservation 65

Brecksville Reservation

After clearing the trees, sections of this reservation were once farmed. Between 1830 and 1840 at least one such farmer, Charles Rich, built a farmhouse and other buildings on what is now the western edge of the reservation. Known as *Squire*, he ran a 65 acre farm, but was also the justice of the peace. The typical western reserve farmhouse is now maintained as a museum by the Brecksville Historical Society.

During the depression federal relief workers built the Brecksville Nature Center as well as other park structures found along the hiking trails. The nature center was completed in 1939, the same year as the heavy forest cutting in the Bradley Woods Reservation (p.26). Near the nature center is the 300 acre Harriet Keeler Memorial Woods. Harriet L. Keeler (1846 - 1921) graduated from the nearby Oberlin College in 1870 and was a conservationist who had written many botanical books. In addition to her love of nature, she was a teacher who served as assistant principal of Cleveland's Central High School for 30 years. Also near the nature center is the *tallgrass prairie restoration project* which is bringing back plants once common to the area.

Brecksville Reservation

Most of this reservation is dominated by the Chippewa Creek Gorge and many ravines. Chippewa Creek is a post glacial stream that cuts through shale and sandstone before it merges with the Cuyahoga River at the eastern end of the reservation. However, there are also granite boulders that glaciers once brought here from Canadian mountains. Seven ravines were also cut by streams trying to reach the Cuyahoga River.

The resulting topography creates a variety of forests among which can be found twenty different species of ferns. The trees are represented by oak and hickory found on dry ridge tops. Beech and maple (some over 200 years old) are found on moist slopes. Cottonwoods, Sycamores and Willows are found in the flood plains. Also, on some of the steep north slopes are eastern hemlocks. These are remnants of the cooler climate glacial period forests.

Merging near the very interesting sandstone formations of what is known as Deer Lick Cave (a large sandstone overhang) are two limbs of the Buckeye Trail (p. 64). This famous trail encircles Ohio with the Medina and Akron segments merging in Brecksville, then continuing north through the Bedford (p. 72, 76), South Chagrin (p. 88, 92), and North Chagrin (p. 96, 98) Reservations. The Medina segment also crosses the Hinkley Reservation (p. 56, 60). Of additional historic interest are the remnants of the Ohio Canal along Towpath Hiking Trail. This trail is in the northeastern part of the reservation and follows the old Ohio and Erie Canal towpaths just east of the Cuyahoga River.

Brecksville Reservation

Bedford Reservation

Acquired:	1920's
Size:	2,154 Acres
Location:	16 miles southeast of downtown Cleveland
Features:	Golf Course
	Bridle Trail
	All-Purpose Trail
	Hiking Trail
	Physical Fitness Trail
	Baseball Diamond
	Sledding
Water Resource:	Tinker's Creek
Terrain:	Deep Gorge
	Thick woods with stands of large trees

Bedford Reservation

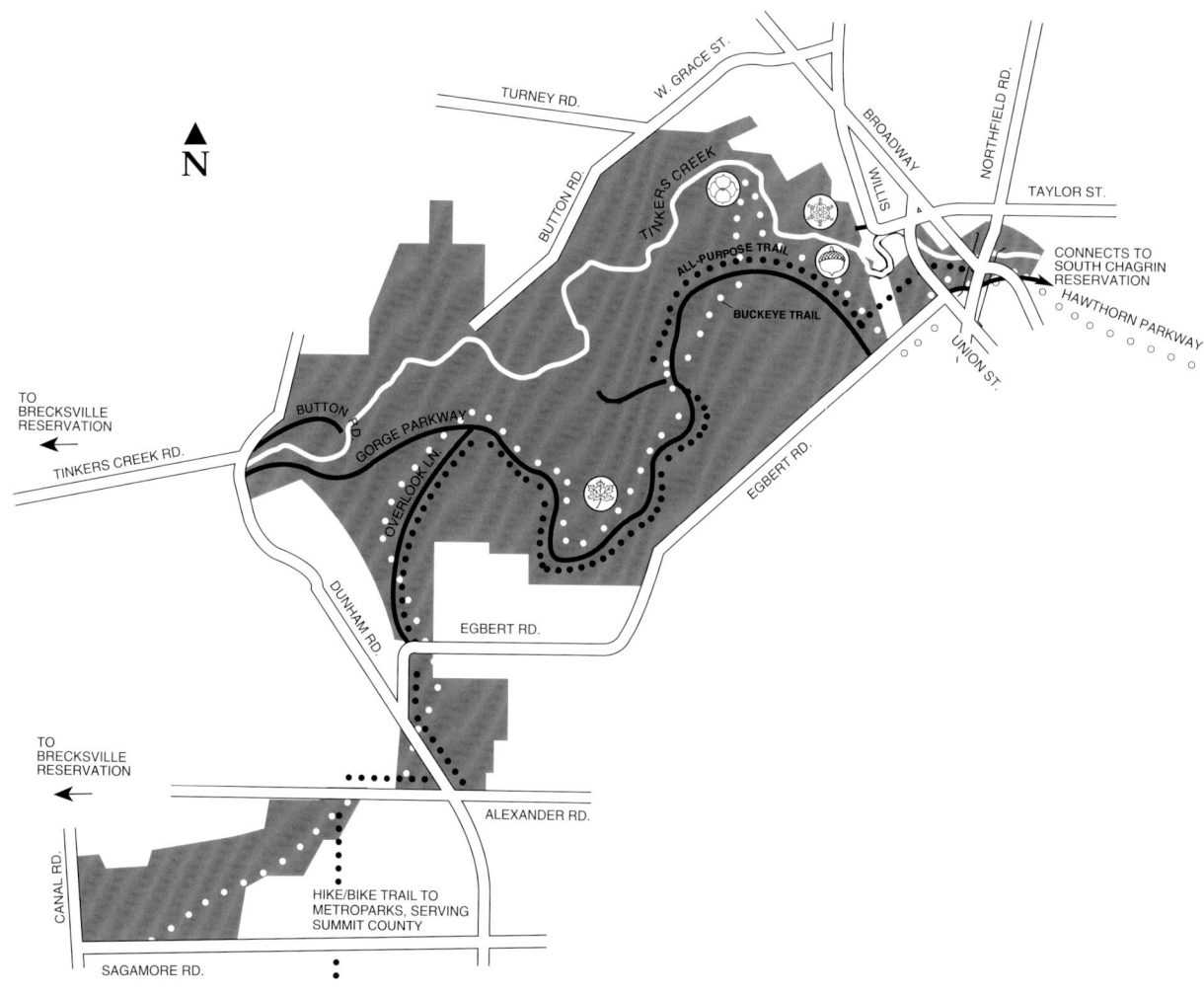

Bedford Reservation 73

Bedford Reservation

This reservation is perhaps best known for Tinker's Creek Gorge which was designated a National Natural Landmark in 1968. Tinker's Creek was named after a member of Moses Cleaveland's surveying party. On its two mile length through the reservation, it drops 200 feet, carving a steep gorge that reveals geologic stratifications of the past 300 million years. Exposed formations include Berea sandstone, Bedford shale and sandstone, Cleveland shale, and Chagrin shale. The Bedford Formation was first described here and is designated a "type locality." Also unique to the gorge area are 29 different species of native trees with unique nitches from ridge tops to flood plains.

Tinker's Creek winds through the park hitting directly against the gorge wall at nine different points. Its fast waters were power for a woolen mill built by Stephen Powers in 1842 and operated for 15 years. The water was also used for a grist mill and chair factory.

Bedford Reservation

Other interesting area history includes a Moravian missionary settlement founded in 1786 at the junction of Tinker's Creek and the Cuyahoga River. It was called Pilgerruh or *Pilgrim's Rest*. Also, along the northern border of the reservation is Button Road. Laid out in 1801, it was one of the early pioneer roads. Though not confirmed, it may have been one of the old locations of a great Indian path of Ohio, the Mohoning Trail. However, a portion of the Buckeye Trail (p. 72) does run through this reservation. The Buckeye Trail extends from Cincinnati at the Ohio River to Headlands State Park on Lake Erie and in the process also traverses the Hinkley (p. 56, 60), Brecksville (p. 64, 68), South Chagrin (p. 88, 92), and North Chagrin (p. 96, 98) Reservations. Declared a state trail in 1971, it is broken into approximately 24 segments with maps and information on each segment available through the Buckeye Trail Association, Inc. (p. 133). At this time the only Metropark maps that show the trail are those of the Brecksville and North Chagrin Reservations.

Bedford Reservation

Garfield Park Reservation

Acquired:	1986
Size:	177 Acres
Location:	12 miles southeast of downtown Cleveland
Features:	Nature Center Hiking Trail Baseball Diamond
Water Resource:	Mill Creek Wolf Creek
Terrain:	High, flat fields Thickly wooded creek valley

Garfield Park Reservation

Garfield Park Reservation

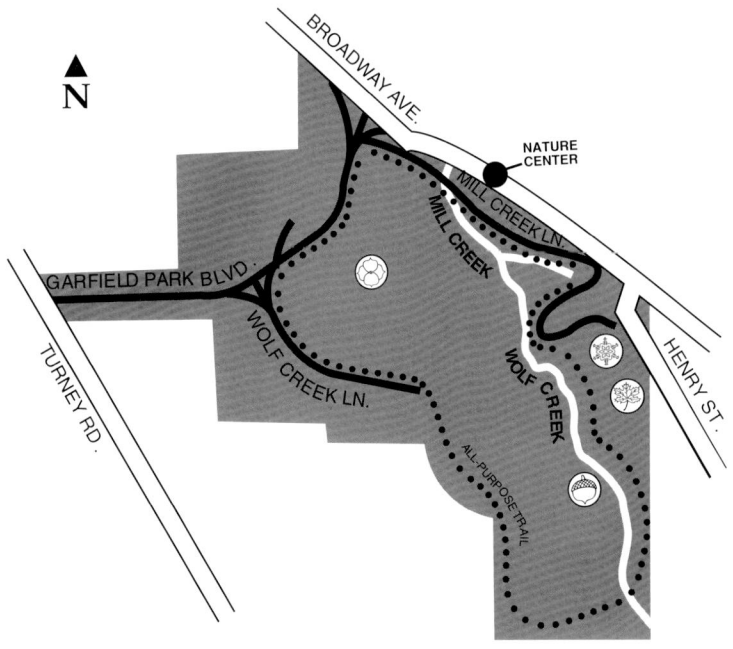

Garfield Park Reservation

Garfield Park Reservation

Ten years prior to Moses Cleaveland's exploration of the shore of the Cuyahoga River and what is now Cleveland, Moravian missionaries created a Christian Indian settlement in the Cuyahoga River Valley. This was in 1786. In 1798, Judge James Kingsbury settled an area east of the Cuyahoga River. This became the Newburgh Township. Located on a ridge, Newburgh became a place to which Clevelanders could escape from their swampy Cuyahoga River. Newburgh and Cleveland both wanted to become the county seat. In the early 1800's Newburgh grew faster than Cleveland, but Cleveland was favored when the Ohio Canal was built in 1827 and a new courthouse was built on Public Square. Parts of Newburgh and Independence Townships eventually became what is now Garfield Heights. The railroads arrived in 1855 and there was rapid growth in what was once an area of small farms.

In 1894, the City of Cleveland bought the Dunham, Rittenberger, and Carter farms. In 1895, the land became Newburgh Park, and in 1897 was renamed Garfield Park.

Garfield Park Reservation

Garfield Park became known for the beauty of its forests, high promontories, and creek valleys. Eventually, electric street cars carried people from Cleveland to enjoy the country and collect mineral spring water. By 1930, visitors could enjoy a boating pond, swimming pool, walking paths, baseball diamond, football fields, and tennis courts. Visitors also came to enjoy the beautiful landscaping and stonework reflecting the influence of Frederick Law Olmsted. Olmsted was a famous landscape architect and park planner. He designed or helped design many of the nation's parks, but is perhaps best known for his planning of New York City's Central Park. In the same year that Garfield Park opened (1895) Olmsted began work on Biltmore, the Vanderbilt estate in North Carolina. This was his last major project and was carried on by his son, Frederick Law Olmsted, Jr., who later helped with the planning of Euclid Creek and Rocky River Reservations (p. 106 and p. 34). Much of the original Garfield Park stonework that Olmsted helped design is still evident today.

Garfield Park Reservation

South Chagrin Reservation

Acquired:	1920's
Size:	1,879 Acres
Location:	14 miles southeast of downtown Cleveland
Features:	Polo Field
	Look About Lodge
	Bridle Trail
	Fishing
	Ice Fishing
	All-Purpose Trail
	Hiking Trail
	Physical Fitness Trail
	Baseball Diamond
	Ice Skating
	Sledding
Water Resource:	Chagrin River
	Sulphur Springs Brook
	Shadow Lake
Terrain:	Deep woods with ravines and hills
	Valley along Chagrin River with high sidewall rock formation and small tributary streams
	Meadows at north end

South Chagrin Reservation

South Chagrin Reservation

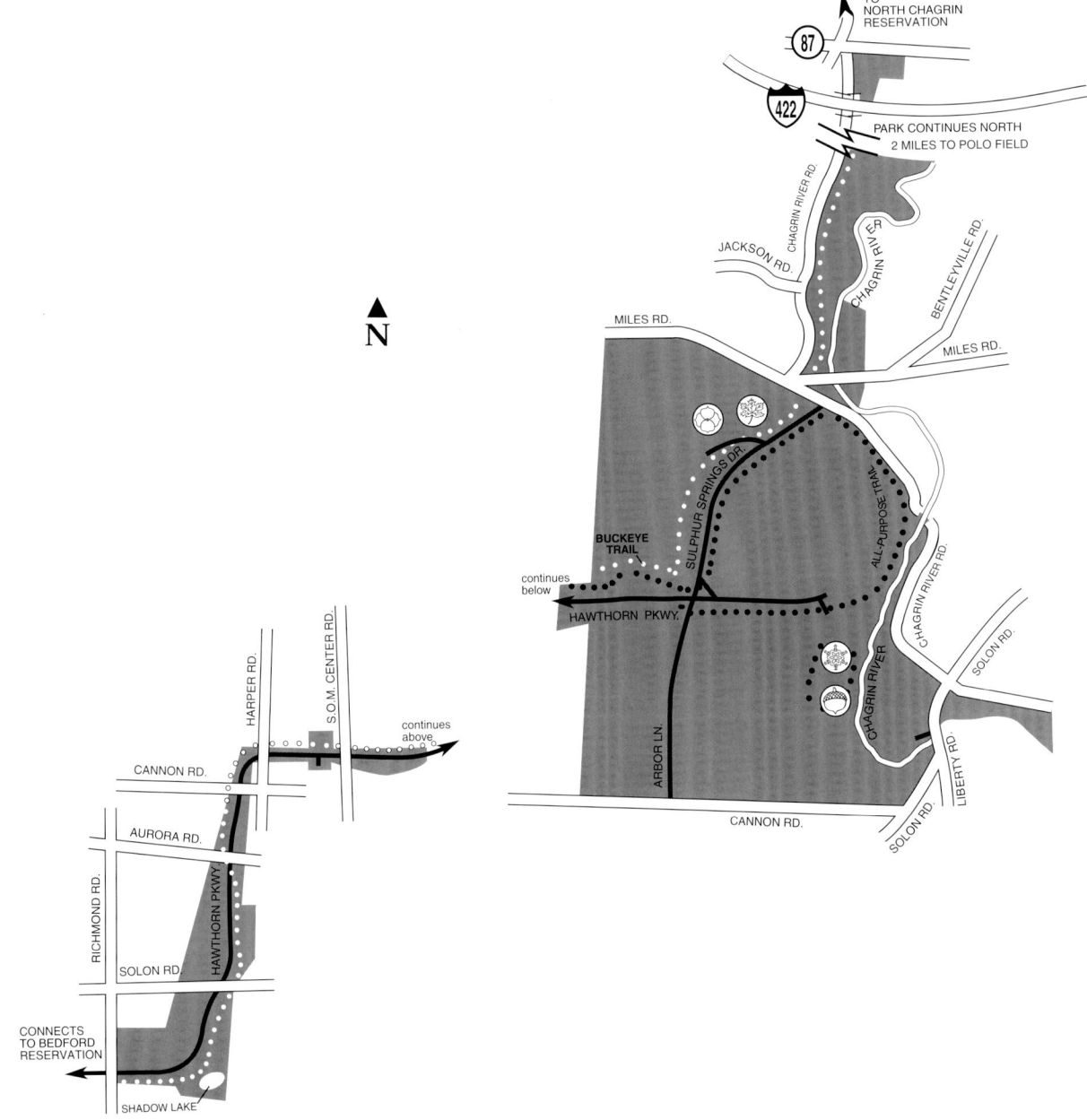

South Chagrin Reservation

South Chagrin Reservation

A pioneer industry once existed here based on quarrying Berea sandstone for grindstones and whetstones. Evidence of the quarry can be found at the Quarry Rock picnic area at the southeast end of the reservation. However, Squaw Rock is the best known historical landmark of this reservation. This large sandstone boulder, also in the southeastern end of the reservation, is found along the Chagrin River. What makes it interesting are the carvings of a Chagrin Falls blacksmith, Harry Church (1836 - 1908). In 1885, Church carved the reliefs of a squaw, rattlesnake, quiver of arrows, and an infant in swaddling clothes on one side of the rock easily seen from a hiking path. On another side, facing the river, are carved the likeness of the White House and a log cabin. It is said that Church titled the rock, *The Rape of the Indians*, but its true significance is unknown. Church was a spiritualist who recorded his own funeral oration, sculpted his own tombstone, and is said to have been a painter and musician as well. As a historical reference point it is interesting to note that Church did his carvings 5 - 10 years prior to when Mr. Squire was trying to build his estate in what is now the North Chagrin Reservation. Also, 60 years later Mr. Stuart was carving figures in the sandstone of the Hinkley Reservation (p. 58).

South Chagrin Reservation

Squaw Rock is found along a hiking trail built in 1931 — 32. The trail follows the west bank of the river below large rocky overhangs and boulders with several small streams and waterfalls flowing into the Chagrin River. Stone steps take one down below these rocky walls to the trail at the rivers' edge.

Further north is Sulphur Springs Brook which flows through a hemlock woods and is stocked with brook trout. Even further north are Look About Lodge (headquarters of the Cleveland Natural Science Club) and several meadows. The meadows are used for bluebird nesting sites that have been maintained by volunteers ever since the 1970's. At the most northern section of the reservation are the polo fields which are used for polo matches as well as dog and horse shows.

In 1967, the reservation was enlarged with the addition of a former boy scout camp at its southern end. One can still find a fishing pond on this land that vastly increased the size of the reservation.

At the very southern most part of the reservation is the picturesque Shadow Lake. Created in 1962, it is used for fishing and ice skating, as well as just a nice walk around its perimeter. The Buckeye Trail skirts the lake on its way north, primarily following the parkway as it heads towards the North Chagrin Reservation and eventually Headlands State Park. For more Buckeye Trail information see the map and history sections of the Hinkley (p. 56, 60), Brecksville (p. 64, 68), Bedford (p. 72, 76), and North Chagrin (p. 96, 98) Reservations.

South Chagrin Reservation

North Chagrin Reservation

Acquired:	1925
Size:	1,912 Acres
Location:	21 miles east of downtown Cleveland
Features:	Trailside Nature Center
	Nature Center and Bookstore
	Waterfowl Sanctuary
	Squires Castle
	Golf Course
	Fishing
	Ice Fishing
	Bridle Trail
	All-Purpose Trail
	Hiking Trail
	Physical Fitness Trail
	Cross Country Ski Rental
	Ice Skating
	Sledding
Water Resource:	Chagrin River
	Oxbow Lagoon
	Sunset Pond
	Strawberry Pond
	Sanctuary Marsh
	Buttermilk Falls
Terrain:	High land, descends east to the Chagrin River
	Thick woods with deep ravines
	Several open playing fields

North Chagrin Reservation

North Chagrin Reservation

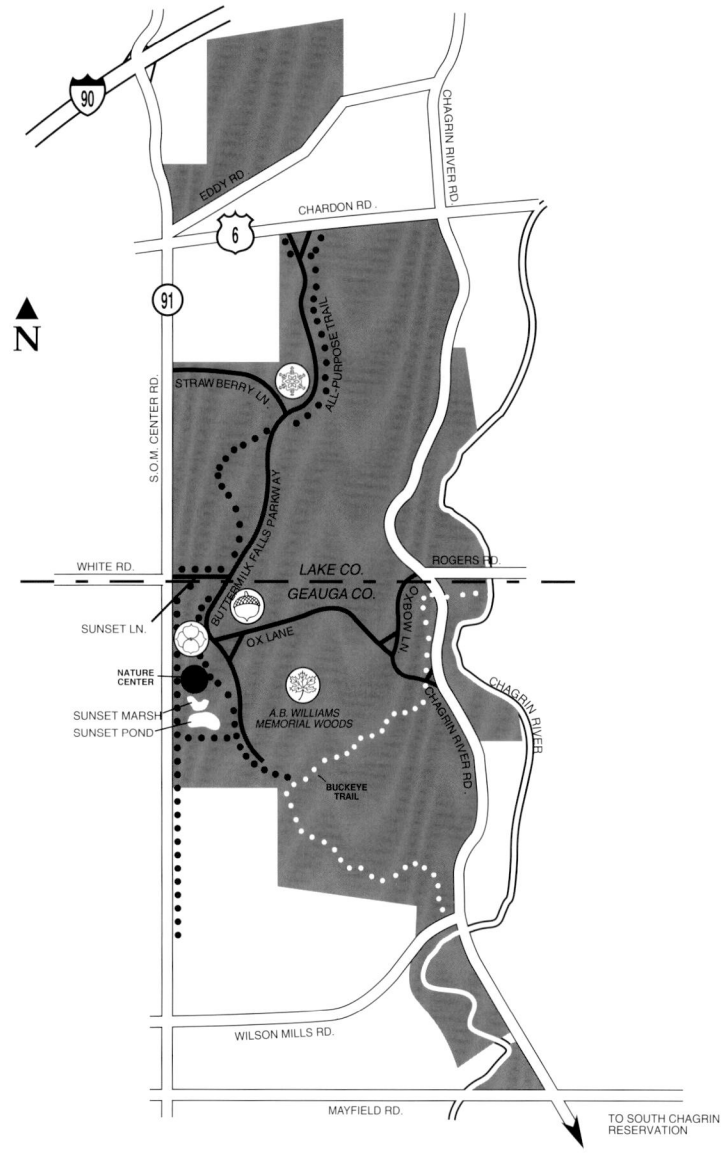

North Chagrin Reservation

North Chagrin Reservation

North Chagrin Reservation had its beginning with 525 acres of land on which still stands Squire's Castle. Fearus B. Squire (1850 - 1932) was vice-president of Standard Oil Company. In the 1890's he began accumulating land and building an estate in the Chagrin Valley. Squire's Castle is actually the gatehouse of the planned estate which Mr. Squire named *River Farm*. The "Castle" is styled after English or German baronial halls and built of stones quarried on the land. Never finishing the project, eight miles of gravel roads and a pond were built before selling the land in 1922. It was purchased for the Metroparks in 1925.

On its way north a portion of the Buckeye Trail traverses the North Chagrin Reservation (p. 96). Founded in 1959 as a way to link the Ohio River with Lake Erie, it loops throughout the state while passing through parks as well as developed land. Also known as the *Blue Blazes Trail* it is marked by blue markers which in the case of developed regions might even be found on telephone poles! Additional reservations traversed by this trail include Hinkley (p. 56, 60), Brecksville (p. 64, 68), Bedford (p. 72,76), and South Chagrin (p. 88, 92).

North Chagrin Reservation

On 65 acres of this reservation is a beech-maple climax forest. A climax forest is one that has been unaltered and has reached its fullest natural development to date. Before Cleveland was even founded, this area was known for its many deer, wild turkeys, wildcats, and wolves. The woods has been designated the *Arthur B. Williams Memorial Woods* for the Metroparks' first interpretive naturalist. Visiting the woods weekly from 1932 - 1935, Mr. Williams noted 393 plant species and 170 animal species. However, since the original study many more species have also been added to the list. The first trailside nature center in the Metroparks was in these woods and opened July 4, 1931. Though the nature center was struck by lightning and destroyed by fire in late 1980's the woods remain on the National Register of Historic Places.

Also of interest is a stand of white pines found on the White Pine Loop Trail. A wood used for ship masts in the 19th century, this is the oldest remaining stand of white pines in Cleveland.

A large number of waterfowl can be found in the two-acre marsh of the Sanctuary Marsh Wildlife Preserve. However, another wetland, *The Swamp*, is also home to numerous birds such as woodpeckers and swallows. It is found in the lower level, Chagrin River portion of the reservation and is one of the largest swamp habitats in the Metropolitan Parks.

North Chagrin Reservation

Euclid Creek Reservation

Acquired:	1920's
Size:	345 Acres
Location:	12 miles east of downtown Cleveland
Features:	All-Purpose Trail
	Hiking Trail
	Physical Fitness Trail
	Baseball Diamond
	Sledding
Water Resource:	Euclid Creek
Terrain:	Deep wooded gorge
	Downhill course, south to north
	Open field, north end

Euclid Creek Reservation　　103

Euclid Creek Reservation

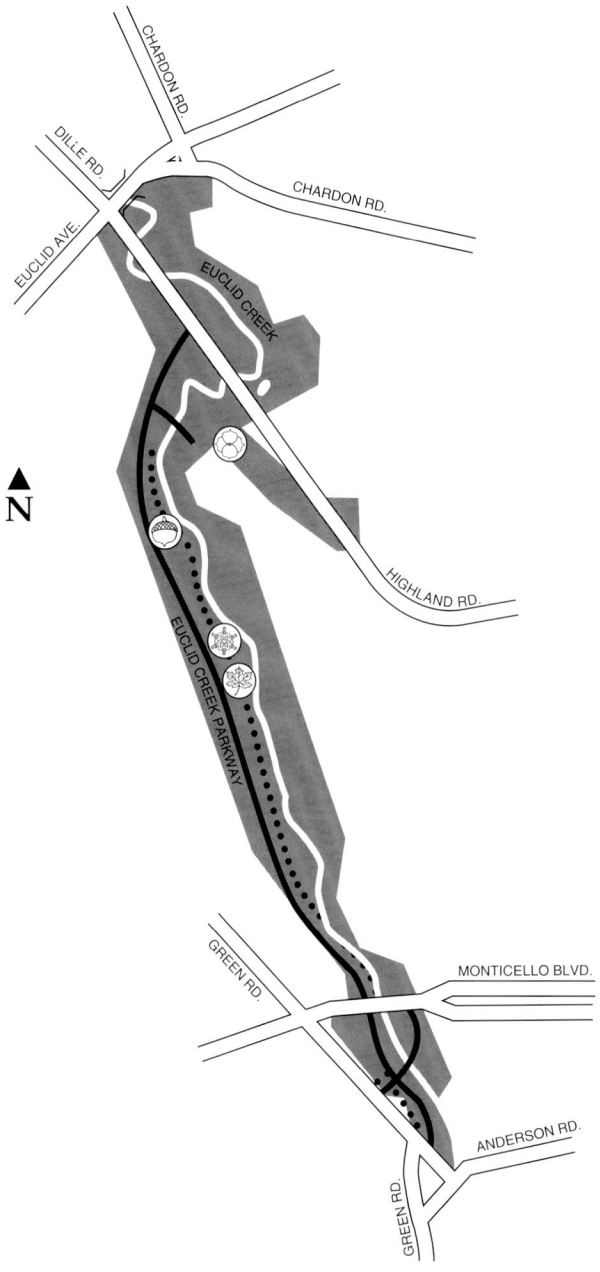

Euclid Creek Reservation

Euclid Creek Reservation

Euclid Creek Reservation is one of the first scenic valleys the Metroparks Board of Commissioners included in their development plan of 1917. Two years prior to this, in September 1915, the well-known landscape architect, Frederick Law Olmsted, Jr., explored the valley. Travelling by foot and photographing the scenery for several days, he praised its natural beauty. He found it well suited for a park and urged that it be preserved in its entirety. He also conferred on ways to acquire land.

Beginning in 1919 and extending through the 1920's, land was acquired primarily from the Cleveland Stone Quarry, as well as the Euclid Stone and Brick Company. The area produced a high-grade, dense, sandstone with a fine grain of blue-grey color known as Bluestone. It was used extensively for Cleveland's sidewalks. Remaining evidence of the era is seen at the southern end of the reservation in the quarry picnic area. The town of Bluestone grew in the late 1800's through the early 1900's, until the introduction of concrete ended the quarries.

From 1933 to 1942, the civilian conservation corps built eight bridges, a shelter house, retaining walls, and a two mile parkway running the length of the reservation. The old quarries were again a source stone for many of the walls and bridges built in the 1930's.

Euclid Creek Reservation

Euclid Creek Reservation is a large gorge carved by Euclid Creek on its way to Lake Erie. In places, the walls rise at least 100 feet above the creek bed and expose layers of Berea sandstone, Bedford shale and sandstone, Cleveland shale, and Chagrin shale. The gorge runs a noticeable downhill course from its southern to northern end and is heavily wooded throughout most of its length. As with several other parks in the Emerald Necklace, Euclid Creek Reservation is surrounded by development and supports wildlife that has had to relocate due to a decreasing amount of "wild" or natural land.

Euclid Creek Reservation

Metroparks Zoo

Founded:	1882 — Wade Park
	1907 — Brookside Park
Size:	165 Acres
Location:	6 miles south of downtown Cleveland
Features:	3,300 Animals
	500 Species
	Rain Forest
	Book & Gift Store
Water Resource:	Big Creek
Terrain:	Rolling hills
	Wooded
	Big Creek Valley

Metroparks Zoo 111

Metroparks Zoo

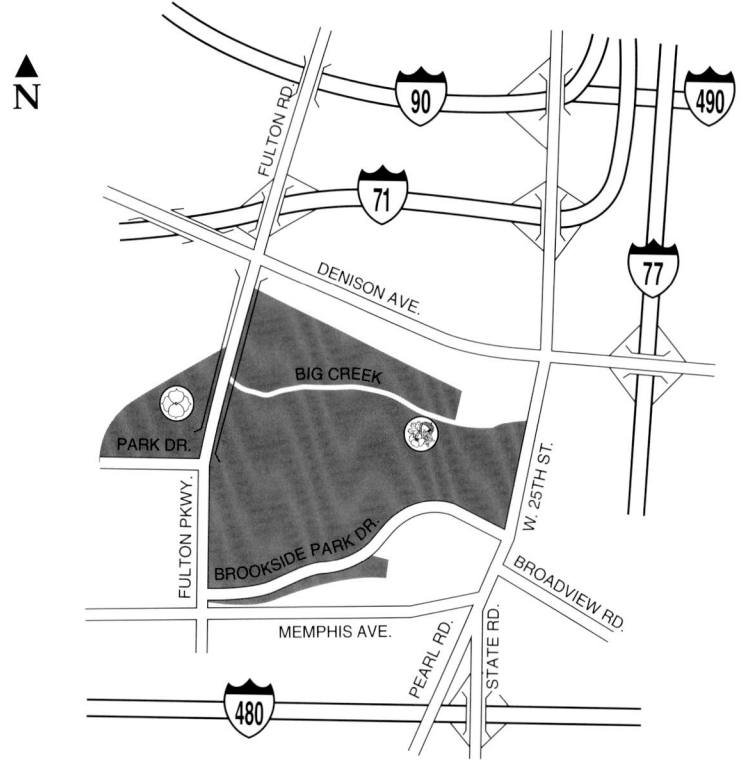

Metroparks Zoo

Metroparks Zoo

The zoo began in Wade Park on September 15, 1882, when Jeptha H. Wade gave a herd of deer and 64 acres of land to the City of Cleveland. Most of the subsequent animals of this early zoo were donated by Cleveland Citizens. A few, such as the lion cubs *Columbus* and *Cleveland*, came from circuses. A tropical animal and bird building came in 1890, and bear pits in 1903.

However, Mr. Wade had also donated three and one half acres of land for what became the Cleveland Museum of Art. As the museum plans grew, it was decided to move the zoo to its present location at Brookside Park. This was a recommendation of William Stinchcomb, Chief Engineer of the City Parks. He was impressed with the scenic beauty of Big Creek Valley and the opportunity the land offered for unusual exhibits. The first building was erected in 1907, but it was not until 1914 that the Wade Park Zoo closed. In 1970, the Wade Park deer barn, the only remaining structure of the original zoo, was moved to the Brookside Park site. Also in 1970, zoo ownership transferred to the Cleveland Metropolitan Park District.

Metroparks Zoo

There was great expansion of the zoo while operated by the Cleveland Museum of Natural History from 1940 — 1957. (Of note is the 1955 Zoo West Africa Expedition led by F. C. Crawford as well as Gordon and Vernon Stouffer). There was continued expansion from 1957 — 1975 when operated by the Cleveland Zoological Society. Since 1975, operations have been by Cleveland Metroparks with emphasis on natural settings. In 1986, the zoo acquired the Cleveland Aquarium collection.

At a cost of $30 million and covering 87,000 square feet is the newest addition to the zoo, the *Rain Forest*. Enclosed in a split-level domed structure kept at 80°F are approximately 600 animals of 118 species, 300 reptiles of 50 species, and 7,000 plants of 360 different varieties and 65 plant families. Opened in 1992, it offers an education as to the importance of rain forests with representation of all three of the major tropical rain forests; African, Asian, and South American.

Metroparks Zoo

Artist's Statement

My goal in photography is to capture the essence of a scene at the peak decisive moment that may last minutes, or only seconds, but produces the image we remember and equate with an entire experience. There are moments in all our lives that are fleeting yet representative of feelings we remember forever. It is ironic that as photographers we take these brief moments and then do all that we can to make them permanent! Nevertheless, if done well the final product will engage and "capture" the viewer as much as the photographer has captured the image and all that it represented.

To produce these images a photographer has primarily a camera to work with. Many people view the camera as synonymous with "photography," but it is only a tool, just as the paint brush is to a painter. The production of a photograph does not even begin with the camera, but rather with the recognition of the image. This recognition may require seeing a scene mentally as though through a long lens, or require an unusual widening of the senses to realize one is actually in the *middle* of the scene. *This* is the beginning of a photograph. The rest is a matter of mental gymnastics and hard labor. It involves mobilizing oneself, and quite often, perservance.

Once a decision has been made to photograph a scene there is much to do in what is often a short space of time. With this in mind I have often said that good landscape photography is every bit as much "action" photography as a sports event. Many scenes must be anticipated, while others can never be anticipated but meteorically appear unannounced. In any event these scenes may only last an instant. To capture the essence of the moment and make it look as we perceived it is a constant struggle.

In the past I have found that many people were as interested in what went on during the creation of a photograph, both logistically and mentally, as they were in the end product. Therefore, for your enjoyment the following pages include a synopsis on the making of each image. They are grouped by park reservations with image identification correlated to the seasonality symbol. In the text of the book these symbols can also be found on the appropriate reservation maps to indicate the general area in which the image was discovered.

Technical Data

Camera:	Hasselblad 500CM and 503CX
Lenses:	Zeiss 40mm, 80mm, 150mm, 350mm
Film:	Kodachrome 64, Fujichrome 50, Ektachrome 64X
Prints:	Cibachrome Glossy

I use a medium format camera because of the larger image than that of a 35mm camera, and hence a more satisfying appearance of large prints. I would like to use a large format camera but have compromised for the convenience of roll film. The lenses most often used are the 80mm and 150mm. The lens I like the best is the 150mm.

All photographs (as opposed to the lithographic reproductions in this book) are Cibachrome prints. Though the Cibachrome dye-bleach process can be problematic due to its high contrast, it is preferred because of its archival qualities, high color saturation, and extreme clarity. For me, it helps produce a feeling of being able to walk into the scene. Since the transparency is only a middle point in the photographic process, all images in this book were color separated from Cibachrome prints, the final embodiment of the image at its best.

Huntington Reservation

While photographing, I look up as much as anything else. In every reservation I visited, I found at least one abstract pattern of branches worthy of photographing. I liked this one because the birch tree appeared as a design woven through a darker and finer background pattern, all on a blue cloth of sky. I tried several different vantage points before settling on this one.

After getting up in the dark in order to catch the sunrise over Lake Erie, I slowly woke up with lots of coffee and by working through several scenes. After the sun had risen more, I fell in love with this isolated tree by Lake Erie. It really made a statement. The only difficult part of this photograph was getting the sun in the right position with some interesting clouds before it rose out of the scene. Afterwards, I was awake but couldn't wait to take a shower and get breakfast. For this image I owe thanks to my assistant who was also willing to get up early and encouraged me not to put off doing the "sunrise on Lake Erie" that I knew I wanted but never got around to doing.

I liked the mosaic patterns in this scene. I'd found it during the summer, but came back in fall when the leaves would add just a little more character to the pattern. I liked the leaning tree bisecting the square and adding some tension or energy to the scene. However, this was a relaxing image to get because I knew just what I wanted and where I was going. Also, it was a beautiful fall day.

One image of the Huntington Reservation had to have was these old concrete supports for railway trestles. Now mingled in with an overgrown woods, they have the appearance of an ancient temple being reclaimed by nature. In winter, they have an appearance of bleached tree trunks. There were other images showing more of the supports, but I liked the way these blended into the scene. My assistant was eager to get on to other parks as I seemed to be spending an inordinate amount of time with this scene. However, as it turned out, the last image was the best image.

Bradley Woods Reservation

Several people over two days stopped and asked with surprise and curiosity what I was photographing. Affectionately called *the mud pond*, I was intent on seeing the sky by looking down! The clear air, blue sky, and small green leaves near the tree trunk were as much spring as were flowers in bloom. To get this image looking the way it "felt" I had to scrape the pond clear of debri which, once photographed, would take on ghastly, distracting proportions.

Many of the images in this book were taken at the end of my hikes through any given reservation. At about 4:00 p.m. on a July 4th I was set up waiting for some dark clouds to pass when I looked to my right and saw this scene, *The Pathway Out*. It has a nice beckoning quality raising the question of "what's beyond the bend in the shadows?" Afterward I went home to watch the Edgewater Park fireworks.

This is literally the last image of the day. I'd spent all afternoon photographing some very nice scenes when I decided I needed more lakes in the book. The setting sun and reflected yellows in the water were a perfect fall feel. But the sun was very intermittent. My first photograph was not well illuminated. Almost to the car, more sun came out and I raced back to perfect the image. While walking back to the car a horrible thought crossed my mind that I may not have used the correct camera settings. When the sun came out a third and last time, I raced back to get the final image.

This was one of the first scenes I saw in this reservation. It was taken just after photographing the winter image used for the nearby Huntington Reservation. I was very pleased to be in time to capture the sun in this image, framed by snow clouds no less. It is the dark clouds that give the drama to the stage set by the tree on the left. This is one of those "action" images where good teamwork with my assistant allowed us to set up before the sun and clouds had irrevocably changed positions. We saw the cloud coming in from the right and fortunately caught it before it covered the sun.

Rocky River Reservation

It had been raining off and on all day. I would wait in the car and even visited my nearby parents while torrents of rain would come down. But it was a good day with three different park areas still captured in the sporatic appearance of sunlight. At the end of the afternoon the sun came out for an extended period of time which is when I saw this scene from the road. I was ecstatic about this one because it had such a feeling of openness and of the clean, cool air one gets in the spring. The river in the foreground is Rocky River.

I'd wanted to take this image for years. With the making of this book, I had a reason to do it. In driving by this spot I've always been impressed with the haunting drop off in perspective and the juxtaposition of a carpet of grass extending up to the fringe of a dark, "wild" woods. It is not easy to reproduce the feeling one gets in a car when a series of images impact the eye from a constantly changing view. After trying several different vantage points, I felt this one most closely approximated the feel I was after.

One of my favorites, this is a stream my cousins and I used to play in as kids. Due to the shale formation around the bend there is a small waterfall we used to call *Little Niagara*. This was taken at sunset and is near the mouth of the stream where it runs into Rocky River. It was taken on one of those great fall days when the sun was out all day and there were images everywhere. A good mood prevailed, and earlier I even had a pleasant conversation from across the river with someone reading a book in the afternoon sun.

With a windchill factor of $-20°$, this was not a fun photograph to take, but I knew I wanted the steep shale cliffs along Rocky River and I didn't know how much longer winter would last. So, along with an assistant we went for it. We had a difficult time handling equipment as we'd already been out all afternoon. She was absolutely frozen, but a real trooper. After this image we took one or two more, then went for hot tea and a Chinese dinner. By then it was dark.

Mill Stream Run Reservation

Before going deep into the woods, I came across this very open scene with lots of light and the yellow green of early spring leaves. The leaves in the foreground are left over from last fall. There was plenty of time to set up the equipment and enjoy the ambience. By summer this will have filled in with dark shadows. I also photographed several abstract and tightly cropped scenes at the same site. However, I liked the openness of this area best. It hints at the vast expanse of woods that does indeed spread out behind it.

While hiking down an almost dry river bed, we found a rather bold crawfish that defiantly raised its claws. Just beyond us was this river bend and cliff. It was a hot day, but it was relatively cool down here and there was a constant breeze that every now and then would stop for a few seconds. I like the way the large trees on top of the cliff give perspective to size of the river bed. Also, I generally like river bends, for they always lure one along to see what else might be hidden from view.

In search of color all day, we were tipped off that Mill Stream Run had good color at its southern end. As the sun was setting, the last rays fell on this tulip tree that seemed to be in constant motion from an approaching storm. The storm turned out to be snow! But by then it was already getting dark. With an umbrella held over the lens we photographed even in the dark. Several impressionistic "winter" scenes were obtained. But no one would have believed they were fall images! Also, I fell in love with the colors and composition in the tulip tree. This scene was found in Stuhr Woods which at the time was part of the Mill Stream Run Reservation, but which has been remapped as part of the Brecksville Reservation.

This is a sunset scene. I had taken a walk in the late afternoon in search of images but without much luck until I found this tributary to Rocky River. If the river had been more frozen it would have been nice to follow the stream into the background hills. I came back the next day to see if I could improve on this image, but in photography, as with many things in life, one rarely gets a second chance. Though all the "characters" were the same, the magical feel was gone on the second visit. The lighting was not as interesting and the river was completely covered in a uniform but boring white snow. I was fortunate to have found the scene the first time.

Big Creek Reservation

There are many cliffs, streams and rivers throughout the park. The spring sun on these cliffs and the budding leaves made a nice contrast. I knew I wanted an image of these cliffs and the creek, but took an hour to find the right vantage point. Then I had to wait by the creek's edge while someone finished crossing the water. During all this I was hoping the sun would not change too much and was lucky that the soft glow remained long enough for a good photograph.

Lake Isaac Waterfowl Sanctuary has a great abundance of birds. Birds are very hard to photograph artistically and I didn't have the patience for the many ducks behind me and at my feet. My assistant was a friend who had just flown in from Los Angeles and we were looking forward to a restful dinner. Hence, I probably opted for this typical hot summer day scene with its play of light and shadow because of its serene appearance. After all, it is the feeling of serenity that probably entices us to feed and watch waterfowl in the first place!

The fall of 1992 was *very* rainey and cold. I had spent several weeks trying to get the image I *thought* I wanted for Big Creek, a scene with lots of rocks and beech trees. I had taken many photographs while waiting for the sun, but it never appeared. Finally, I found this scene by accident while taking an exploration hike through the woods to just relax. There were virtually no leaves left on the trees, and it was cold. The sun came out for about 30 seconds just as I had set up for this photograph. It was a good scene in dim light, but the sun really brought out the textures.

It was a freezing cold, but very sunny day. As I hiked up this hill, I almost stepped into the scene which would have ruined the pristine appearance. I spent another two hours getting other images, but couldn't beat the strong lines found here, forming rectangular and square patterns within the larger square.

Hinkley Reservation

There were fields of trillium in bloom on this warm and sunny day. After taking many different photographs of both close up and wide angle views of the trillium, I settled on this one because of its openness and lush greens. It was a great day with several scattered and brief rain storms. I even rushed down to the lake in hopes of catching a storm cloud over the water, but was too late. In any event, it probably would not have matched this image as a representation of spring.

A classic summer image of late afternoon corn fields at Buzzard Roost where the buzzards return to Hinkley every spring. I was being attacked by swarms of mosquitoes while taking this image. My assistant and I were putting on all the repellent we could find, but the mosquitoes always found places we missed. Just after this, we finally photographed the corn fields from a different vantage point but which didn't have the strong contrasts found here. Then the camera jammed and we ended up taking an hour to just hike and find vantage points for a return trip.

I knew I wanted rock formations at Whipp's Ledges. With an assistant I spent almost all day climbing the fantasy-like world of crevices, cliffs, and large boulders of rock. Since it was a beautiful sunny day, it is ironic that I liked this end-of-the-day image best. We called it *the Battleship* because of the large rock on the right. The left wall is a favorite with rock climbers. Taken late in the day long after everyone else had left, this was an approximately two minute exposure.

This was the last image of winter I had to obtain, and almost missed it. It was late winter, possibly the exact last day, when I got up early to get to Hinkley. The ice was already melting on the lake, and by the time I finished, it had melted completely. I photographed a great abstract ice pattern in the shore of the lake, but chose this image for the book because I wanted trees in each scene. That afternoon, though it was technically winter, I roamed the park in 60 degree weather and obtained some very unique images due to the position of the sun and the lack of snow.

Brecksville Reservation

This is another end-of-the-day image in the rain. After half an afternoon of photographing in the rain, the setting sun backlit this intriguing scene taken from an all purpose trail. It seemed to exemplify the misty, wet feel I had all day. Also, the leaves were growing quickly and by summer, as with the spring image of Mill Stream Run Reservation, this would be a mass of dark shadows. I felt I had found a unique moment. Cold and wet, I then went to a nearby deli for a club sandwich and a satisfying ride home, in the rain.

I was by myself this time, and was also carrying some new equipment (and hating every minute of it). A *very* hot day with sweat dripping from every pore in my body did not make this intimate scene any cooler. The wide range of light to dark, and constant motion in the leaves, made it difficult to think through and execute this photograph. Also, the sun kept changing. It is the sun on the leaves and their halo-like affect that really creates this scene. After this I took some images of the falls further downstream and had a pleasant talk with someone visiting from Florida.

A classic image from a lookout point, this is only one of two images in the book with a man made structure in it. However, the bridge in the upper right is stone, blends with the scene, and makes a nice "knot" pulling all the elements together. I tried leaving the bridge out, but the image lost all it's power. I set out specifically to get this image and was afraid I'd miss all the color. The leaves were rapidly falling and being blown off the trees even as I photographed. I used a polarizer on this one to enhance the color, but had to choose a setting that would not eliminate all the wonderful play of light on the rocks and creek below.

A very close call! I almost decided to just head home from photographing Bedford, as I was cold and the sun was setting. I decided since it took so long to get a quality image, it was worth making a run for Brecksville to see what might be there. After taking a wrong turn and loosing time, the adrenalin was building as I raced toward Brecksville, not even knowing where I was specifically going! As the sun was literally dropping out of sight, I found this very nice faint glow on trees seen from across a field. Talking to myself and rushing to the field's center, I got this image *just* in time. Afterward I had my traditional very satisfying club sandwich from a nearby deli. This time I'd played the game, gambled, and won.

Bedford Reservation

This is a special photo taken at sunset at the bottom of a long descent to Tinker's Creek. A low trillium flower just beyond a nearby tree trunk seemed as something out of a fairy tale, as though it had magical powers to dispel a curse and produce a prince or princess. It was a 60 second exposure and difficult to get without motion. I was very worried I wouldn't get out okay, because I didn't bring a flash light and it was getting very dark. However, even if I had to crawl out, I wanted this image.

I was more intrigued by the shadow of the tree trunk than Bridal Veil Falls itself. It was a quiet end of the day with the last ray of sun making a stand. Because of the sun dial effect of the tree trunk, the scene shifted quickly. Hence, this could be considered an "action" photo. Five minutes earlier I had just lost a similar image further downstream because I was too slow. The small stream in the lower right balances the curve of the shadow but is only a tiny portion of the falls.

The leaves were just beginning to turn color and yet some trees had already lost their leaves. Taken in late evening, Ektachrome Plus helped spark up this scene. There is a shear cliff just beyond the dark cherry tree trunk. There is nothing beyond it but a straight drop into Tinker's Creek gorge. My assistant took a while to adjust to the precarious perch and kept warning me not to get too close to the edge. However, I had to position the cherry tree trunk in an exact position for this image, and with a little prudence was able to capture the feel one had while being there.

There are several paths along this side of Tinker's Creek gorge. I had actually scouted this site on an earlier visit after I had, embarrassingly and aggravatingly, run out of film. Originally the scene was to be photographed from below. However, on a warm winter day I ended up perched on a cliff overhang. I wanted the sun on the rocks and icicles, but it only appeared intermittently. In the meantime, I was trying to make sure I or my equipment didn't roll off the rock on which I was crouched. Incidentally, there is a *much* larger drop off to the right of this scene.

Garfield Park Reservation

I knew I wanted this dogwood tree as a classic symbol of spring. What sets it off is the powerful tree trunk next to the dogwood tree in bloom. All that remained to do was find the right composition. It's nice now and then to find such a straight forward in-the-open, scene.

This was definitely an action scene. A sudden and passing rain storm, combined with a setting sun, did not allow much time to set up. My assistant and I were running across the field trying different vantage points. We stayed until dark photographing other interesting scenes as well, but I liked the energy embodied in this one. Cleveland is well known for its sudden rain storms.

Classic Fall — This is what we all want as photographers, hikers and dreamers; a quiet pool of water, small falls, and an umbrella of color. The leaves in the foreground couldn't have been placed any better. It is a restful scene, and my assistant and I took the opportunity to relax ourselves while waiting for the right light. Actually, I ran out of film at one point and she had to go back for more while I guarded the equipment. I was standing on a rock in the middle of the stream and didn't want to set up for this image a second time. It was hard enough finding a stable rock to begin with.

The first scene I saw on my first ever visit to Garfield Park Reservation was this huge oak tree in the middle a snow fall which had big, slowly falling, fluffy snowflakes. It was great while it lasted. Just like the winter image in North Chagrin, the magic was gone when the full sun came out and the snow stopped. Without an assistant for this one, it was difficult to keep the rapidly accumulating snow off the lens. The snow came down so fast that when I turned around the camera bag had a good layer of snow on it.

South Chagrin Reservation

This could almost pass for a green summer image. The tip-off that it is spring is the lush light green at the end of the hemlock trees. Also, though one would not know simply by viewing the image, the sun casts this type of light on the rock only at this time of year. This was not an "action" photo in that there was no harsh beam of light that often moves like a sundial and changes the scene by the minute. Instead, I was dealing with broader swaths of soft, filtered light. I found this scene at the end of a long hike after spending much time photographing the scene I thought for *sure* I'd use. However, the symmetry of this scene with the interplay of soft and hard edges and subtle lighting was a must have!

I knew ever since spring that I wanted this scene for my summer image. I used Kodachrome film for the more blue-green tones of a late summer day. I could not have made the image without the help of an assistant to pull branches out of the viewing angle. I liked the sense of a special place, not only as a plateau, but as a small peninsula. It took nature so long to carve this "gem" of a place that I'm glad there is no picnic table here to ruin the image!

The fall weather in 1992 was very unusual. It rained and even snowed. Classic fall colors were difficult to find in artistic settings. I was planning on these leaves being at this waterfall, and was delighted at the carpet of yellow. However, I spent about an hour at this site trying to compose the image and then waiting for the right light which would only last about 30 seconds at a time. Near the end of a cold, rainy day, these were long exposures that brightened up with the use of Ektachrome or Fujichrome. The long exposure, however, produced a problem. There was constant tree motion or leaves falling into the image area causing a blur. Timing was critical on this one.

It was an extremely cold, brittle day when my assistant and I set up for this image. We were relatively protected by this rocky overhang, but the coldness and hardness of the rocks seemed to exemplify the day. I was impressed with the tenacity of the trees hanging on the rocky edges and felt we were similarly just trying to get through a cold day. However, the trees had much more practice and were doing a better job of it, while we merely endeavored to stay warm and avoid frost bite.

North Chagrin Reservation

Especially in Cleveland, the seasons can have great overlap in their appearance. In early spring there was still snow at Buttermilk Falls. After spending about twenty minutes trying to find an engaging vantage point, I decided the small gorge was more interesting than the falls. I believe the strength of this image is the layering of levels from the green moss in the foreground to the old snow melting in an abstract appearance of the gorge. It took several takes to get one without too much motion in last year's leaves still hanging onto the beach tree.

This is another one of those unexpected scenes that took some quick action to get. After spending an hour photographing a large scale scene, I packed up. Then I saw this perfect little composition that was right behind me all the time. Also, it did not last long because the sun soon shifted and the entire scene became too dark. It was a tantalizing image because the sun would quickly come and go even as I composed the image.

After spending half a day in the rain looking for classic fall color and only photographing pine trees while my assistant held an umbrella over the equipment, we stumbled on this scene. After taking what I thought was the best possible photograph, I took my assisstant to lunch which I'd promised her for an hour. But I *had* to go back. More sun had come out. Combined with the softening mist of heavy rains, I got the fall color, and the uniqueness, I was after. The rain had also darkened the tree trunks for a nice touch of contrast.

This is a scene I fell in love with from the road. In the last days of winter on a warm morning there was fog intermittently rolling through the park. The almost Japanese-type design of the arching pine tree and thawing lake was unbelievable. I had to get this one *fast*. The fog was very inconsistent and the sun soon became very bright, dispelling the mystic quality of the image and, instead, creating a trite picture postcard look.

Euclid Creek Reservation

Having already captured a recognizable winter landscape further south in the park, I was looking forward to complete freedom at the north end of the park for my spring image. I spent a full morning by myself hiking around and getting some nice images. The winning photograph was, as is often the case, the *last* image I saw as I was hiking back down a hill. Believe it or not, this was an action shot. I had to work fast to keep the line of light below the dark rain clouds. It's the slight tension created by this line of light matched by the light bark of a small beach tree (protected and consuming its space in the foreground) that makes this a one of a kind image.

After spending a morning photographing abstract water and rock patterns, after photographing Euclid Creek in a summer version of an area I eventually used as the winter scene, and after talking to a gentlemen from Florida who was visiting his grandson, I saw this. It simply said *Summer*; dark green with dark cool shadows. This was a relatively easy image to photograph. It was slightly more difficult to print to keep the detail in the darker shadows while not burning out the bright spots.

This is a great example of finding the image within the image. Late in the day and after photographing this scene many different ways it finally fell into place by backing up and using a 300mm lens. The resulting image is the intimate look I felt while there, the invitation to walk into the woods. I'm glad not all the leaves had changed color yet. It makes a bolder statement as it is. This was almost the last image of the day, but just after this we moved further south and took images even after it was dark. These later images were very good, but did not have this fall look to them.

This was a rather straight forward scene I knew I wanted. Seen from near a parking lot it is easy to get to and has classic lines. I was lucky the sun was bright and at just the right angle for some interesting shadows and for a nice sparkle on the water. Ironically, there was very little snow in the park that day as it was near the end of winter. But I like the scene better than if the creek had been buried in snow.

Metroparks Zoo

How does one photograph a zoo without being cute, or trite? I settled on these spring flowers and early leaf buds against the Fulton Bridge which takes cars across the valley and the zoo. The landscaping is as much a part of the zoo experience as is the wildlife. Quite often visitors would stop to say the scene I was working on was very beautiful.

The last three images of the zoo were all taken in the Rain Forest. Hence, there is no special season as we know it that can be attached to them. As it was, I went to the Rain Forest during one of Cleveland's worst snow storms. I wasn't sure this was the best thing to do when the radio kept telling people to stay home, but felt the Rain Forest would be empty and I'd get my best vantage points! On the way home there were roads closed and at one point live wires sparking and falling in front of me. But I had that good feeling photographers have when they know they've captured on film the image they had wanted.

Front Cover

As the cover image of the book I am not releasing the particular reservation where I found this scene. It symbolizes the entire park, in that I found beech and maple trees, and at least one large, old oak tree in every reservation. This scene was taken while standing on the side of a hill. Hence, the feeling of being up in the trees. I also chose this image because fall is one of my favorite seasons.

Afterward

Since the days of my childhood thoughts about Indians roaming through the *Emerald Necklace* I have matured as a person and as a photographer. While developing my own photographic style I have explored the works of others such as Carleton Watkins from the very early days of photography, the 20th Century "Masters" as Edward Weston, Ansel Adams, and Elliott Porter, and current photographers such as environmentalist Robert Glenn Ketchum. These are just a few of those who have contributed to the exploration of our lands and to the furtherment of landscape photography as an art form. I have come to appreciate that just as the land is a continuum with each parcel inexorably linked to the next, so is the time in which we experience it. I am honored to have had the opportunity to record and interpret some of our local landscapes that with time have passed through many changes and have been inhabited by so many before us. One can only view with respect those remnants of older landscapes that link our land and our time with the past, and realize that what we preserve and create now will be the future links in this continuum. There will always be land. The question is "will there be a place for Nature?"

I hope you have found your journey through *Gems of the Necklace* to have had moments of anticipation as well as reflection, not only of the site imaged, but maybe of other life experiences linked to the outdoors and nature. I hope I have awakened or strengthened your concern for *any* natural setting worthy of preservation.

Lastly, whether you prefer *The Park*, *The Valley*, or *The Emerald Necklace*, I hope you will visit it often, explore areas you've never been, and, as the current guardians, treat it kindly. ∎

References

Cleveland Metroparks Past and Present
  Book by Carol Poh Miller
Cleveland Metroparks — Your Special Place
  Essays by Kathleen Hempker
Park Brochures: *Step Back In Time . . . Garfield Park*
  Garfield Park
  The Buzzards of Hinkley
  Fort Hill
Cleveland Metroparks Naturescape, A Visitor Guide
The Rain Forest / Cleveland Metroparks Zoo
  Press Release and Bulletins
Stuart's Folk Art Legacies Carved in Stone Are Washing Away
  The Plain Dealer, May 23, 1993 — Article by Karen Farkas
Cleveland Metroparks, A Supplement to Cleveland Magazine
  Cleveland Magazine, July 1992 — Article by Lee Melius
Cleveland's Jewel Celebrates 75th Anniversary
  The Plain Dealer, January 12, 1992 — Article by Pauline Thoma
A Guide To The Cleveland Metroparks System
  Road and Reservation Maps.
Fifty Hikes In Ohio
  Book by Ralph Ramey
Great Quotes from Great Leaders
  Book by Great Quotations Publishing Co.
Emerald Necklace
  Metroparks Newsletter
Follow the Blue Blazes
  Maps — Buckeye Trail
Posted Signs along Park Reservation Paths

National Association For Olmsted Parks
National Park Service, Frederick Law Olmsted National Historical Site
Baycrafters Art Gallery
Metropark Nature Centers and Naturalists
Case Western Reserve University, Department of Anthropology
The Cleveland Museum of Natural History, Department of Archaeology
Personal documentation through site visits

Buckeye Trail showing the areas covered by each section map.

Metroparks Administrative Office	(216) 351-6300
Brecksville Nature Center	526-1012
Garfield Park Nature Center	341-3152
Rocky River Nature Center	734-6660
Sanctuary Marsh Nature Center	473-3370
Metroparks Zoo	661-6500
Earth Words Bookshop	449-0511
Bentleyville Historical Society	247-5546
Brecksville Historical Society	526-6757
Hinkley Historical Society	278-2154
Olmsted Historical Society	777-0059
Baycrafters Art Gallery	871-6543

Buckeye Trail Association, Inc.
P.O. Box 254
Worthington, Ohio 43085

Metroparks Administrative Office
4101 Fulton Parkway
Cleveland, Ohio 44144

To order books by mail, for a brochure of Marmolya Cleveland skyline posters and limited edition lithographs, or for tear sheets on a Chicago skyline or Banff, Canada, scenic mountain poster, contact:

Photographs Elite
12700 Lake Avenue, Suite 2005
Lakewood, Ohio 44107 U.S.A.
(216) 228-6640

For Cibachrome Photographs contact Peter Wach:

The Wach Gallery
31860 Walker Road
Avon Lake, Ohio 44012, U.S.A.
(216) 933-2780

The beginning . . . .

An early effort in my exploration of nature photography, the above image depicts a tree that was a familiar landmark during childhood adventures in the Rocky River valley.